weightwatchers360°

D0019118

Veg
Power!

weightwatchers360°

Veg Power!

140 recipes to pump up produce, use less meat

**Weight Watchers
Publishing Group**

VP, Editorial Director **Nancy Gagliardi**

Creative Director **Ed Melnitsky**

Photo Director **Deborah Hardt**

Managing Editor **Diane Pavia**

Assistant Editor **Katerina Gkionis**

Food Editor **Eileen Runyan**

Editor **Jackie Mills, R.D.**

Nutrition Consultant **U. Beate Krinke**

Recipe Developers **Adrienne Anderson,
Lori Longbotham, Michele Peters,
Jackie Plant, Michael Tyrell**

Production Manager **Alan Biederman**

Photographer **Rita Maas**

Food Stylist **Toni Brogan**

Prop Stylist **Megan Hedgpeth**

Art Director **Amy Trombat**

Designer **Liz Trovato**

**Copyright © 2013 Weight Watchers
International, Inc.**

**Nothing may be reprinted in whole or in part
without permission from the publisher.
Editorial and art produced by W/W
Twentyfirst Corp., 11 Madison Avenue,**
New York, NY 10010.
**WEIGHT WATCHERS is a registered
trademark of Weight Watchers
International, Inc.
SKU #11983 Printed in the USA**

Front cover: Summer Rolls with Chili-Garlic
Dipping Sauce, page 38.
Back cover: Vegetable Crêpes with Tomato
Sauce (page 155), Grilled Tofu Kebabs with
Pineapple Sauce (page 78), Grilled Pizza with
Gouda and Kale (page 133).

about Weight Watchers

Weight Watchers International, Inc. is the world's leading provider of weight-management services, operating globally through a network of company-owned and franchise operations. Weight Watchers holds nearly 45,000 meetings each week worldwide, at which members receive group support and education about healthful eating patterns, behavior modification, and physical activity. Weight-loss and weight-management results vary by individual. We recommend that you attend Weight Watchers meetings to benefit from the supportive environment and follow the comprehensive Weight Watchers program, which includes a food plan, an activity plan, and a behavioral component.

WeightWatchers.com provides subscription weight management products, such as eTools and Weight Watchers Mobile, and is the leading internet-based weight management provider in the world. In addition, Weight Watchers offers a wide range of products, publications (including **Weight Watchers Magazine** which is available on newsstands and in Weight Watchers meeting rooms), and programs for people interested in weight loss and control. For the Weight Watchers meeting nearest you, call **1-800-651-6000**. For information about bringing Weight Watchers to your workplace, call **1-800-8AT-WORK**.

**SMOKY THREE-CHEESE MAC'
AND CHEESE, PAGE 54**

contents

chapter 1
breakfasts with staying power
Kick-start your day in a healthful way with these filling and wholesome
morning meals.

chapter 2
satisfying lunches
Fuel up for the afternoon with delicious sandwiches, soups,
salads, and more.

chapter 3
stick-to-your-ribs dinners
Cook hearty, healthy meals the whole family will love.

chapter 4
tastes like chicken
Use non-meat substitutes to create iconic dishes usually made
with chicken.

chapter 5
slow cooker favorites
Bring comfort with soups, stews, chilis, and tagines.

**QUINOA AND ROASTED VEGETABLE SALAD,
PAGE 63**

about our recipes

While losing weight isn't only about what you eat, Weight Watchers realizes the critical role it plays in your success and overall good health. That's why our philosophy is to offer great-tasting, easy recipes that are nutritious as well as delicious. We make every attempt to use wholesome ingredients and to ensure that our recipes fall within the recommendations of the U.S. Dietary Guidelines for Americans for a diet that promotes health and reduces the risk for disease. If you have special dietary needs, consult with your health-care professional for advice on a diet that is best for you, then adapt these recipes to meet your specific nutritional needs.

To achieve these good-health goals and get the maximum satisfaction from the foods you eat, we suggest you keep the following information in mind while preparing our recipes:

WEIGHT WATCHERS 360° AND GOOD NUTRITION

■ Recipes in this book have been developed for Weight Watchers members who are following Weight Watchers 360°. *PointsPlus*® values are given for each recipe. They're assigned based on the amount of protein (grams), carbohydrates (grams), fat (grams), and fiber (grams) contained in a single serving of a recipe.

■ Recipes include approximate nutritional information; they are analyzed for Calories (Cal), Total Fat, Saturated Fat (Sat Fat), Trans Fat, Cholesterol (Chol), Sodium (Sod), Carbohydrates (Carb), Sugar, Dietary Fiber (Fib), Protein (Prot), and Calcium (Calc). The nutritional values are calculated by registered dietitians, using nutrition analysis software.

■ Substitutions made to the ingredients will alter the per-serving nutritional information and may affect the *PointsPlus* value.

■ Our recipes meet Weight Watchers Good Health Guidelines for eating lean proteins and fiber-rich whole grains, and for having at least five servings of vegetables and fruits and two servings of low-fat or fat-free dairy products a day, while limiting your intake of saturated fat, sugar, and sodium.

■ Health agencies recommend limiting sodium intake. To stay in line with this recommendation we keep sodium levels in our recipes reasonably low; to boost flavor, we often include fresh herbs or a squeeze of citrus instead of salt. If you don't have to restrict your sodium, feel free to add a touch more salt as desired.

▥ In the recipes, a green triangle (▲) indicates Weight Watchers® Power Foods.

▥ Stay On Track suggestions have a *PointsPlus* value of **0** unless otherwise stated.

▥ Recipes that work with the Simply Filling technique are listed on page 193. Find more details about this technique at your meeting.

For information about the science behind lasting weight loss and more, please visit **WeightWatchers.com/science.**

PointsPlus VALUE NOT WHAT YOU EXPECTED?

You might expect some of the *PointsPlus* values in this book to be lower when some of the foods they're made from, such as fruits and vegetables, have no *PointsPlus* values. Fruit and veggies have no *PointsPlus* values when served as a snack or part of a meal, like a cup of berries with a sandwich. But if these foods are part of a recipe, their fiber and nutrient content are incorporated into the recipe calculations. These nutrients can affect the *PointsPlus* value.

▥ Alcohol is included in our *PointsPlus* calculations. Because alcohol information is generally not included on nutrition labels, it's not an option to include when using the hand calculator or the online calculator. But since we include alcohol information that we get from our nutritionists you might notice discrepancies between the *PointsPlus* values you see in our recipes, and the values you get using the calculator. The *PointsPlus* values listed for our recipes are the most accurate values.

SHOPPING FOR INGREDIENTS

As you learn to eat healthier and add more Power Foods to your meals, remember these tips for choosing foods wisely:

LEAN MEATS AND POULTRY

Purchase lean meats and poultry, and trim them of all visible fat before cooking. When poultry is cooked with the skin on, we recommend removing the skin before eating. Nutritional information for recipes that include meat, poultry, and fish is based on cooked, skinless boneless portions (unless otherwise stated), with the fat trimmed.

SEAFOOD Whenever possible, our recipes call for seafood that is sustainable and deemed the most healthful for human consumption so that your choice of seafood is not only good for the oceans but also good for you. For more information about the best seafood choices and to download a pocket guide, go to **environmentaldefensefund.org** or **montereybayaquarium.org.** For information about mercury and seafood go to **weightwatchers.com.**

PRODUCE For best flavor, maximum nutrient content, and the lowest prices, buy fresh, local produce, such as vegetables, leafy greens, and fruits in season. Rinse them thoroughly before using and keep a supply of cut-up vegetables and fruits in your refrigerator for convenient, healthy snacks.

WHOLE GRAINS Explore your market for whole-grain products such as whole wheat and whole-grain breads and pastas, brown rice, bulgur, barley, cornmeal, whole wheat couscous, oats, and quinoa to enjoy with your meals.

PREPARATION AND MEASURING

READ THE RECIPE Take a couple of minutes to read through the ingredients and directions before you start to prepare a recipe. This will prevent you from discovering midway through that you don't have an important ingredient or that a recipe requires several hours of marinating. And it's also a good idea to assemble all ingredients and utensils within easy reach before you begin a recipe.

WEIGHING AND MEASURING The success of any recipe depends on accurate weighing and measuring. The effectiveness of the Weight Watchers program and the accuracy of the nutritional analysis depend on correct measuring as well. Use the following techniques:

■ Weigh food such as meat, poultry, and fish on a food scale.

■ To measure liquids, use a standard glass or plastic measuring cup placed on a level surface. For amounts less than $\frac{1}{4}$ cup, use standard measuring spoons.

■ To measure dry ingredients, use metal or plastic measuring cups that come in $\frac{1}{4}$-, $\frac{1}{3}$-, $\frac{1}{2}$-, and 1-cup sizes. Fill the appropriate cup and level it with the flat edge of a knife or spatula. For amounts less than $\frac{1}{4}$ cup, use standard measuring spoons.

GRILLED PIZZA WITH GOUDA AND KALE, PAGE 133

introduction

If you'd like to enjoy the healthful benefits of a vegetarian diet, but you're not ready to give up meat, this book is for you! You don't have to become a strict vegetarian to start eating more plant-based meals that are wholesome, packed with flavor, and nutritious. In this cookbook, we give you a bounty of ideas for healthy no-fuss meals with no meat—and a variety of recipes where adding some meat is optional. All are satisfying, filling, and delicious.

Good for you. Replacing some of the high fat meat in your diet with beans, soy products, whole grains, fruits, and vegetables means you'll consume more fiber, antioxidants, vitamins, and minerals. And this plant-based diet means a healthier you—some research has found that people who eat less meat have a lower incidence of colon cancer and type 2 diabetes. The best news of all: Researchers have found that people who eat very little or no meat have significantly lower body weights than those who eat meat.

You can still get enough protein. Eating less meat will not make you deficient in this vital nutrient as long as you replace it with plant-based protein rich foods. A woman needs only 46 grams of protein each day and a man needs 56 grams. You'll get 8 grams from an 8 ounce glass of fat-free milk, 13 grams from a cup of cooked dried beans, 26 grams from a 3-ounce serving of chicken breast, and 13 grams from an egg. Foods like grains, pasta, breads, and even vegetables have small amounts of protein that add to your total intake over a day. There's no need to worry about combining different foods in each meal to get a "complete" protein, even if you're a strict vegetarian. If you're eating a varied diet with plant-based protein every day, you will meet your protein needs.

Take small steps. If you're a pure carnivore and love meat at every meal, start by eating one of our meatless meals from this book each week, and slowly work your way up to one day a week without meat. No matter where you are on the carnivore to vegetarian spectrum, as you introduce more meatless meals into your eating plan, you can still cook the favorite dishes you love—like pasta, pot pie, and chili—using vegetarian recipes. Try our Tempeh and Mushroom Bolognese with Fettuccine, page 83, Chickpea Pot Pie, page 96, or Chipotle Lentil Chili with Brown Rice, page 108. You don't have to make drastic changes to the way you eat or sacrifice enjoying your favorite foods.

chapter 1
breakfasts with staying power

crispy grits with egg and tomato scramble

serves 4

1 cup water
½ cup low-fat (1%) milk
¼ teaspoon salt
▲ ⅓ cup quick-cooking grits
¼ cup shredded reduced-fat Cheddar cheese
2 teaspoons olive oil
▲ 2 tablespoons minced onion
▲ 1 medium tomato, chopped
▲ 3 large eggs
▲ 3 large egg whites
½ teaspoon chopped fresh thyme
⅛ teaspoon black pepper

1 Lightly spray 8-inch square baking pan with nonstick spray.

2 Combine water, milk, and ⅛ teaspoon salt in medium saucepan; bring to boil over medium-high heat. Gradually whisk in grits. Reduce heat to low and cook, stirring frequently, until grits are thick and smooth, about 5 minutes. Remove from heat and stir in 2 tablespoons Cheddar. Spread grits evenly into prepared pan; let stand until set, about 10 minutes. Cut grits into 8 squares.

3 Heat 1 teaspoon olive oil in large nonstick skillet over medium heat. Add grits squares and cook until lightly browned, turning once, 8–10 minutes.

4 Meanwhile, heat remaining 1 teaspoon oil in second large nonstick skillet over medium heat. Add onion and cook, stirring occasionally, until softened, 5 minutes. Add tomato and cook, stirring occasionally, until softened, 3 minutes.

5 Whisk together eggs, egg whites, thyme, pepper, and remaining ⅛ teaspoon salt in medium bowl. Add egg mixture to skillet and scramble until set but still moist, 2–3 minutes. Serve egg scramble with grits squares. Sprinkle with remaining 2 tablespoons Cheddar.

Per serving (2 grits squares with ½ cup egg mixture): 180 Cal, 8 g Total Fat, 3 g Sat Fat, 0 g Trans Fat, 146 mg Chol, 315 mg Sod, 14 g Carb, 3 g Sugar, 1 g Fib, 12 g Prot, 117 mg Calc.

CAN'T COMMIT? Add 4 ounces chopped fully cooked chicken sausage along with the onion in step 4. The per-serving **PointsPlus** value will increase by **1**.

CRISPY GRITS WITH EGG
AND TOMATO SCRAMBLE

roasted pepper quiche with brown rice crust

serves 6

▲ **1½ cups cooked brown rice**

▲ **1 large egg white**

▲ **1 cup fat-free egg substitute**

▲ **¾ cup fat-free half-and-half**

½ cup shredded part-skim mozzarella cheese

▲ **⅓ cup roasted red bell pepper (not oil-packed), drained and chopped**

¼ cup kalamata olives, pitted and chopped

⅛ teaspoon black pepper

1 Preheat oven to 375°F. Spray 9-inch glass pie plate with nonstick spray.

2 Stir together rice and egg white in medium bowl; press mixture evenly onto bottom and side of prepared plate. Bake until crust begins to crisp, 10 minutes.

3 Meanwhile, whisk together egg substitute and half-and-half in medium bowl; stir in mozzarella, bell pepper, olives, and black pepper. Pour egg mixture into crust and bake until quiche is golden brown and slightly puffed, 25–30 minutes. Let stand 10 minutes before serving. Cut quiche into 6 wedges.

Per serving (1 wedge): 132 Cal, 3 g Total Fat, 1 g Sat Fat, 0 g Trans Fat, 7 mg Chol, 263 mg Sod, 16 g Carb, 3 g Sugar, 2 g Fib, 9 g Prot, 176 mg Calc.

STAY ON TRACK Serve the quiche for brunch accompanied with wedges of honeydew or cantaloupe melon.

migas
with charro
beans

serves 4 ready in 20 minutes or less

- 1 (15-ounce) can pinto beans, rinsed and drained
- 1 small red onion, chopped
- 1 jalapeño pepper, seeded and minced
- 1 garlic clove, minced
- ½ cup water
- ½ teaspoon salt
- ⅛ teaspoon black pepper
- 2 teaspoons canola oil
- 2 (6-inch) corn tortillas, cut into thin strips
- 4 large eggs
- 2 large egg whites
- 4 tablespoons fat-free pico de gallo

1 Combine beans, onion, jalapeño, garlic, water, and salt in medium saucepan. Cover and cook over medium heat until onion is tender, 10–12 minutes. Stir in black pepper.

2 Meanwhile, heat oil in medium nonstick skillet over medium heat. Add tortilla strips; cook, stirring often, until tortilla strips are browned, 6–8 minutes. Using slotted spoon, transfer to plate lined with paper towels and let drain.

3 Whisk together eggs and egg whites in medium bowl; add to same skillet. Scramble until set but still moist, 2–3 minutes. Gently stir in tortilla strips.

4 Divide egg mixture among 4 plates; top evenly with pico de gallo. Serve with beans.

Per serving (½ cup egg mixture, ⅓ cup beans, and 1 tablespoon pico de gallo): 247 Cal, 8 g Total Fat, 2 g Sat Fat, 0 g Trans Fat, 187 mg Chol, 551 mg Sod, 28 g Carb, 2 g Sugar, 8 g Fib, 16 g Prot, 78 mg Calc.

CAN'T COMMIT? Remove the casings and crumble ¼ pound fresh chorizo. Cook with the tortilla strips in step 2. The per-serving *PointsPlus* value will increase by *2*.

sweet potato and kale frittata

serves 4

- ▲ **3 large eggs**
- ▲ **3 large egg whites**
- **1 tablespoon low-fat (1%) milk**
- **¼ teaspoon salt**
- **⅛ teaspoon black pepper**
- ▲ **1 medium sweet potato, peeled and diced**
- **2 tablespoons plus ¼ cup water**
- **2 teaspoons olive oil**
- ▲ **2 tablespoons finely chopped onion**
- ▲ **3 cups chopped kale**
- **1 tablespoon grated Parmesan cheese**

1 Preheat broiler.

2 Meanwhile, whisk together eggs, egg whites, milk, salt, and pepper in medium bowl; set aside.

3 Combine sweet potato and 2 tablespoons water in small microwavable bowl. Cover with wax paper and microwave on High until softened, 3 minutes. Drain.

4 Heat 1 teaspoon oil in large ovenproof nonstick skillet over medium heat. Add sweet potato and cook, stirring occasionally, until lightly browned, about 3 minutes. Transfer to plate.

5 Add remaining 1 teaspoon oil to skillet. Add onion and cook, stirring often, until onion begins to soften, about 2 minutes. Stir in kale and remaining ¼ cup water. Cover and cook, stirring occasionally, until kale is tender, 8 minutes.

6 Return sweet potato to skillet. Pour egg mixture evenly over vegetables. Cook, lifting edges frequently with spatula to let any uncooked egg flow underneath, until eggs are almost set, about 4 minutes. Sprinkle with Parmesan.

7 Place skillet under broiler 5 inches from heat and cook until eggs are set and top is lightly browned, 2–3 minutes. Cut into 4 wedges.

Per serving (1 wedge): 153 Cal, 7 g Total Fat, 2 g Sat Fat, 0 g Trans Fat, 141 mg Chol, 298 mg Sod, 12 g Carb, 3 g Sugar, 2 g Fib, 11 g Prot, 127 mg Calc.

banana and buckwheat pancakes

serves 4

½ cup all-purpose flour
¼ cup buckwheat flour
½ teaspoon baking powder
⅛ teaspoon salt
½ cup low-fat (1%) milk
2 teaspoons butter, melted
▲ 1 large egg, separated
¼ teaspoon vanilla extract
▲ 1 large egg white
1 tablespoon sugar
▲ 1 small banana, chopped
2 teaspoons canola oil

1 Combine all-purpose and buckwheat flours, baking powder, and salt in medium bowl. Whisk together milk, butter, egg yolk, and vanilla in second medium bowl.

2 With electric mixer on high speed, beat egg whites in third medium bowl until soft peaks form. Gradually beat in sugar until stiff peaks form. Set aside.

3 Add milk mixture to flour mixture, stirring just until blended. Gently fold beaten egg whites into batter just until no streaks of white remain. Fold in banana.

4 Coat large nonstick skillet or griddle with ½ teaspoon oil and set over medium heat. Add batter by rounded tablespoonfuls and cook, in batches, turning once, until golden brown, 6–8 minutes. Transfer pancakes to plate and repeat with remaining oil and batter to make a total of 16 pancakes.

Per serving (4 pancakes): 191 Cal, 6 g Total Fat, 2 g Sat Fat, 0 g Trans Fat, 53 mg Chol, 193 mg Sod, 28 g Carb, 8 g Sugar, 2 g Fib, 6 g Prot, 86 mg Calc.

CHILAQUILES BAKE

chilaquiles bake

serves 4

- ▲ 1½ cups fat-free egg substitute
- ▲ ⅓ cup canned black beans, rinsed and drained
- ▲ ⅓ cup fat-free salsa verde
-    1 (6-inch) corn tortilla, cut into thin strips
-    ¼ cup shredded low-fat Mexican cheese blend
- ▲ 2 scallions, thinly sliced
-    4 tablespoons plain low-fat Greek yogurt
-    1 tablespoon chopped fresh cilantro

1 Preheat oven to 350°F. Spray 4 (6-ounce) ramekins or custard cups with nonstick spray.

2 Stir together egg substitute, black beans, salsa, tortilla strips, Mexican cheese blend, and scallions in medium bowl. Divide egg mixture evenly among ramekins. Place ramekins on baking sheet and bake until centers are set, 30–35 minutes. Serve with yogurt and cilantro.

Per serving (1 ramekin and 1 tablespoon yogurt): 116 Cal, 2 g Total Fat, 1 g Sat Fat, 0 g Trans Fat, 5 mg Chol, 362 mg Sod, 10 g Carb, 2 g Sugar, 3 g Fib, 14 g Prot, 271 mg Calc.

CAN'T COMMIT? Add 2 strips crumbled crisp-cooked bacon to the egg mixture in step 2. The per-serving **PointsPlus** value will increase by **1**.

gingerbread waffles with apples and pears

serves 4

1 cup plus 2 tablespoons all-purpose flour

½ teaspoon baking powder

¼ teaspoon baking soda

¼ teaspoon ground ginger

¼ teaspoon cinnamon

⅛ teaspoon ground nutmeg

1½ cups low-fat buttermilk

2 tablespoons molasses

2 teaspoons butter, melted

▲ 1 large egg, separated

▲ 1 large egg white

1 tablespoon brown sugar

▲ 1 apple, peeled, cored, and thinly sliced

1 tablespoon pure maple syrup

▲ 1 pear, peeled, cored and thinly sliced

1 Preheat waffle baker according to manufacturer's directions.

2 Combine flour, baking powder, baking soda, ginger, cinnamon, and nutmeg in medium bowl. Whisk together buttermilk, molasses, butter, and egg yolk in second medium bowl.

3 With electric mixer on high speed, beat egg whites in third medium bowl until soft peaks form. Gradually beat in brown sugar until stiff peaks form.

4 Add buttermilk mixture to flour mixture, stirring just until blended. Gently fold beaten egg whites into batter just until no streaks of white remain.

5 When waffle baker is ready, pour one quarter of batter onto center and quickly spread within 1 inch of edges. Close baker and bake as manufacturer directs; do not open until done. Repeat, reheating waffle baker before adding each batch of batter, to make a total of 4 waffles.

6 Meanwhile, combine apple and maple syrup in small microwavable bowl. Cover with wax paper and microwave on High for 2 minutes. Add pear to bowl; cover and microwave on High 1 minute longer. Top waffles evenly with fruit mixture.

Per serving (1 waffle and ⅓ cup fruit mixture): 286 Cal, 4 g Total Fat, 2 g Sat Fat, 0 g Trans Fat, 55 mg Chol, 290 mg Sod, 52 g Carb, 21 g Sugar, 2 g Fib, 9 g Prot, 187 mg Calc.

french toast pudding

serves 4

3 slices whole wheat bread, cut into cubes

2 ounces light cream cheese (Neufchâtel)

▲ ½ cup fat-free egg substitute

▲ ¾ cup fat-free half-and-half

½ cup low-fat (1%) milk

2 tablespoons pure maple syrup

1 teaspoon vanilla extract

½ teaspoon cinnamon

1 Spray 1-quart baking dish with nonstick spray. Arrange bread evenly in prepared dish.

2 Place cream cheese in medium bowl. With electric mixer on medium speed, beat until smooth. Add egg substitute and beat until well blended. Add half-and-half, milk, maple syrup, vanilla, and cinnamon. Beat at low speed until blended. Pour egg substitute mixture evenly over bread. Cover and refrigerate 2 hours or overnight.

3 Preheat oven to 375°F.

4 Uncover dish and bake until pudding is set in center and lightly browned, 25–28 minutes.

Per serving (¼ of pudding): 172 Cal, 5 g Total Fat, 3 g Sat Fat, 0 g Trans Fat, 14 mg Chol, 288 mg Sod, 22 g Carb, 13 g Sugar, 2 g Fib, 9 g Prot, 184 mg Calc.

| **STAY ON TRACK** Fresh fruit is the perfect accompaniment to this comforting breakfast casserole. Try serving it with quartered strawberries tossed with chopped fresh mint.

almond crunch loaf

serves 12

½ cup sugar

⅓ cup plus 2 tablespoons sliced almonds

¾ cup all-purpose flour

▲ ½ cup yellow cornmeal

¼ cup cornstarch

½ teaspoon baking powder

½ teaspoon baking soda

▲ 2 large egg whites

4 tablespoons unsalted butter, softened

1 large egg yolk

▲ 1 (6-ounce) container plain fat-free Greek yogurt

½ teaspoon almond extract

½ cup low-fat (1%) milk

1 Preheat oven to 350°F. Spray 4 x 8-inch loaf pan with nonstick spray.

2 Place 2 tablespoons sugar and ⅓ cup almonds in food processor; process until almonds are finely ground. Add flour, cornmeal, cornstarch, baking powder, and baking soda; pulse to blend.

3 With electric mixer on high speed, beat egg whites in medium bowl until soft peaks form. Gradually beat in 2 tablespoons sugar until stiff peaks form; set aside.

4 With an electric mixer on medium speed, beat butter in large bowl until creamy, about 1 minute. Add remaining ¼ cup sugar and beat until light and fluffy. Beat in egg yolk; then beat in yogurt and almond extract. Reduce speed to low. Alternately add flour mixture and milk, beginning and ending with flour mixture, and beating just until blended. Gently fold beaten egg whites into batter just until no streaks of white remain.

5 Pour batter into prepared pan. Sprinkle top evenly with remaining 2 tablespoons almonds. Bake until toothpick inserted in center comes out clean, 35 minutes. Let cool in pan on rack 10 minutes. Remove from pan and let cool completely on rack. Cut into 12 slices.

Per serving (¹⁄₁₂ of loaf): 170 Cal, 6 g Total Fat, 3 g Sat Fat, 0 g Trans Fat, 26 mg Chol, 95 mg Sod, 24 g Carb, 10 g Sugar, 1 g Fib, 5 g Prot, 55 mg Calc.

steel-cut oats with dates and coconut

serves 2

1½ cups water

▲ ½ cup steel-cut oats

½ cup low-fat (1%) milk

1 tablespoon chopped walnuts, toasted

1 tablespoon chopped dates

1 tablespoon shredded sweetened coconut, toasted

1 Combine water and oats in medium microwavable bowl. Cover with wax paper and microwave on High 3 minutes. Let stand at room temperature 30 minutes. Cover and refrigerate overnight.

2 Add milk to oat mixture; stir to mix well. Cover and microwave on High 3 minutes. Stir; then cover and let stand 10 minutes. Top evenly with walnuts, dates, and coconut.

Per serving (generous ¾ cup): 229 Cal, 7 g Total Fat, 2 g Sat Fat, 0 g Trans Fat, 3 mg Chol, 51 mg Sod, 36 g Carb, 8 g Sugar, 5 g Fib, 8 g Prot, 114 mg Calc.

FYI Steel-cut oats are oats that have been cut into small pieces. Unlike old-fashioned or quick-cooking oats, they have not been rolled, or flattened, so they take longer to cook. This recipe speeds up the process with overnight soaking and cooking in the microwave.

wheat berry breakfast salad

serves 4

- ▲ ½ cup wheat berries
- ¼ teaspoon salt
- ▲ 1 orange, peeled and cut into segments
- ▲ 1 small apple, cored and diced
- ▲ 1 small pear, cored and diced
- ▲ 1 kiwifruit, peeled and diced
- ▲ ½ cup seedless grapes, halved
- ½ teaspoon grated orange zest
- 1 tablespoon lemon juice
- 1 teaspoon chopped fresh mint

1 Bring large pot of water to boil over medium-high heat; stir in wheat berries and salt. Reduce heat and cover. Simmer until berries are tender but still chewy, 45 minutes–1 hour. Drain in colander and rinse under cold running water; drain again.

2 Stir together wheat berries, orange segments, apple, pear, kiwifruit, grapes, orange zest, lemon juice, and mint in medium bowl. Serve at once or cover and refrigerate up to 3 days.

Per serving (½ cup): 158 Cal, 1 g Total Fat, 0 g Sat Fat, 0 g Trans Fat, 0 mg Chol, 154 mg Sod, 38 g Carb, 15 g Sugar, 6 g Fib, 3 g Prot, 40 mg Calc.

STAY ON TRACK Top the salad with ¼ cup plain fat-free yogurt (the per-serving *PointsPlus* value will increase by *1*).

**WHEAT BERRY BREAKFAST
SALAD**

polenta with brown sugar ricotta

serves 4   ready in 20 minutes or less

1 cup low-fat (1%) milk
1 cup water
⅛ teaspoon salt
▲ ½ cup instant polenta
⅔ cup part-skim ricotta cheese
1 tablespoon light brown sugar
½ teaspoon vanilla extract

1 Bring milk, water, and salt to boil in medium saucepan over medium-high heat. Slowly pour in polenta in thin, steady stream, whisking constantly. Cook, whisking constantly, until thick and creamy, 3–5 minutes.

2 Puree ricotta, brown sugar, and vanilla in food processor. Divide polenta among 4 bowls; top evenly with ricotta mixture.

Per serving (½ cup polenta and 3 tablespoons ricotta): 147 Cal, 4 g Total Fat, 2 g Sat Fat, 0 g Trans Fat, 16 mg Chol, 299 mg Sod, 19 g Carb, 7 g Sugar, 1 g Fib, 8 g Prot, 246 mg Calc.

STAY ON TRACK   For a little added crunch, sprinkle 1 tablespoon chopped toasted pecans over each serving of polenta. The per-serving *PointsPlus* value will increase by *1*.

quinoa and oat granola

serves 6

2 tablespoons honey

1 tablespoon canola oil

1 tablespoon light brown sugar

¼ cup ground flaxseeds

2 tablespoons quinoa

1 tablespoon sesame seeds

½ teaspoon cinnamon

⅛ teaspoon ground nutmeg

¾ cup old-fashioned oats

2 tablespoons chopped pecans

¼ cup dried cranberries

2 tablespoons raisins

1 Preheat oven to 325°F. Line large rimmed baking sheet with parchment paper.

2 Stir together honey, oil, brown sugar, flaxseeds, quinoa, sesame seeds, cinnamon, and nutmeg in large bowl until combined. Add oats and stir to coat. Spread mixture evenly onto prepared baking sheet.

3 Bake, stirring occasionally, 15 minutes. Stir in pecans; bake until granola is lightly browned, 5 minutes longer.

4 Cool in pan on wire rack. Stir in cranberries and raisins. The granola can be stored in an airtight container up to 2 weeks.

Per serving (about ⅓ cup): 177 Cal, 8 g Total Fat, 1 g Sat Fat, 0 g Trans Fat, 0 mg Chol, 5 mg Sod, 26 g Carb, 14 g Sugar, 3 g Fib, 3 g Prot, 28 mg Calc.

FYI   Quinoa provides more protein than most other grains, and its protein is a complete protein, which contains all the essential amino acids that our bodies need.

chia breakfast biscotti

serves 15

½ cup packed light brown sugar

⅓ cup walnut pieces

1½ cups white whole wheat flour

¼ cup ground chia seeds

½ teaspoon baking powder

¼ teaspoon baking soda

▲ ¼ cup fat-free egg substitute

2 tablespoons canola oil

1 teaspoon grated orange zest

3 tablespoons orange juice

2 teaspoons vanilla extract

½ cup dried apricots, chopped

⅓ cup whole blanched almonds

⅓ cup dried cranberries

1 Preheat oven to 350°F. Lightly spray large baking sheet with nonstick spray.

2 Place brown sugar and walnuts in food processor; process until walnuts are finely ground. Add flour, chia seeds, baking powder, and baking soda; pulse to combine. Add egg substitute, oil, orange zest and juice, and vanilla. Pulse just until mixture forms dough, 5–6 times. Turn dough onto lightly floured surface; sprinkle with apricots, almonds, and cranberries. Briefly knead until fruit and nuts are evenly incorporated.

3 Shape dough into 15-inch log. Transfer to prepared baking sheet and pat dough gently to flatten slightly. Bake until dough is firm to touch and toothpick inserted into center of log comes out clean, 25–30 minutes. Reduce oven temperature to 325°F.

4 Transfer log to cutting board and let cool 15 minutes. Cut log with serrated knife into ½-inch-thick slices (30 slices). Arrange slices in single layer on baking sheet. Bake biscotti 10 minutes; turn over and bake 10 minutes longer. Cool completely on wire rack; biscotti will crisp as they cool. Store biscotti in airtight container up to 2 weeks.

Per serving (2 biscotti): 153 Cal, 6 g Total Fat, 1 g Sat Fat, 0 g Trans Fat, 0 mg Chol, 49 mg Sod, 23 g Carb, 12 g Sugar, 3 g Fib, 4 g Prot, 51 mg Calc.

fruit and nut energy bars

serves 8

¼ cup water

1 tablespoon ground flaxseeds or chia seeds

½ cup dried figs, chopped

¼ cup chopped walnuts, toasted

¼ cup whole raw almonds, chopped

2 tablespoons dried cranberries

2 tablespoons chopped dried mango

2 tablespoons mini–semisweet chocolate chips

2 tablespoons white whole wheat flour

1 tablespoon light brown sugar

¼ teaspoon baking powder

⅛ teaspoon cinnamon

1 Preheat oven to 325°F. Line 4 x 8-inch loaf pan with foil, extending foil over rim by 2 inches. Spray foil with nonstick spray.

2 Stir together water and flaxseeds in small bowl; let stand 10 minutes.

3 Stir together figs, walnuts, almonds, cranberries, mango, chocolate chips, flour, brown sugar, baking powder, and cinnamon in medium bowl. Add flaxseed mixture and stir until moistened.

4 Press evenly into prepared pan. Bake until firm to touch, 20 minutes. Cool completely in pan on wire rack. Lift from pan using foil as handles; cut into 8 squares.

Per serving (1 square): 119 Cal, 6 g Total Fat, 1 g Sat Fat, 0 g Trans Fat, 0 mg Chol, 19 mg Sod, 16 g Carb, 11 g Sugar, 3 g Fib, 3 g Prot, 47 mg Calc.

▌ FYI Store the bars in an airtight container up to 1 week.

MAPLE-GLAZED OAT CAKES

maple-glazed oat cakes

serves 6

¾ cup all-purpose flour

⅔ cup old-fashioned oats

2 tablespoons light brown sugar

1½ teaspoons baking powder

¼ teaspoon baking soda

⅛ teaspoon salt

4 teaspoons cold unsalted butter

▲ ½ cup plain fat-free Greek yogurt

2 tablespoons low-fat (1%) milk

▲ 1 large egg white

3 tablespoons pecans, toasted and chopped

2 dried apricots, diced

2 tablespoons dried cranberries

2 tablespoons golden raisins

2 tablespoons confectioners' sugar

1 tablespoon pure maple syrup

1 Preheat oven to 375°F. Lightly spray baking sheet with nonstick spray.

2 Whisk together flour, oats, brown sugar, baking powder, baking soda, and salt in medium bowl. With pastry blender, cut in butter until mixture is crumbly.

3 Whisk together yogurt, milk, and egg white in small bowl until smooth. Add yogurt mixture to flour mixture; stir just until moistened. Stir in pecans, apricots, cranberries, and raisins.

4 Turn dough onto floured surface and shape into 2½-inch-diameter log; cut into 6 disks. Place disks, cut side down, onto prepared baking sheet. Bake until cakes are lightly browned, 20 minutes. Cool on wire rack 10 minutes.

5 Meanwhile, to make glaze, combine confectioners' sugar and maple syrup in small bowl and stir until smooth. Drizzle glaze over cakes. Serve warm.

Per serving (1 cake): 211 Cal, 6 g Total Fat, 2 g Sat Fat, 0 g Trans Fat, 7 mg Chol, 223 mg Sod, 35 g Carb, 15 g Sugar, 2 g Fib, 6 g Prot, 94 mg Calc.

chapter 2
satisfying lunches

mozzarella and artichoke pitas

serves 2 ready in 20 minutes or less

▲ 1 (14-ounce) can artichoke hearts, rinsed, drained, and quartered

▲ ½ cup roasted red bell peppers (not oil-packed), sliced

3 ounces bocconcini (small fresh mozzarella balls), each cut in half

¼ cup chopped fresh flat-leaf parsley

1 small shallot, minced

2 tablespoons lemon juice

1 teaspoon capers, drained

½ teaspoon black pepper

2 (6-inch) whole wheat pitas, halved

▲ 4 leaves green leaf lettuce

1 Toss together artichoke hearts, bell peppers, bocconcini, parsley, shallot, lemon juice, capers, and black pepper in large bowl. Let stand 10 minutes.

2 Line each pita half with lettuce leaf and fill evenly with artichoke mixture.

Per serving (2 filled pita halves): 362 Cal, 13 g Total Fat, 6 g Sat Fat, 0 g Trans Fat, 30 mg Chol, 977 mg Sod, 52 g Carb, 9 g Sugar, 16 g Fib, 19 g Prot, 218 mg Calc.

FYI If you can't find bocconcini, use 3 ounces regular fresh mozzarella, cut into ½-inch cubes.

roasted vegetable melts

serves 4

- ▲ **2 cups broccoli florets**
- ▲ **1 red bell pepper, thinly sliced**
- **2 garlic cloves, minced**
- **1 tablespoon chopped fresh thyme or ½ teaspoon dried**
- **¼ teaspoon salt**
- **¼ teaspoon black pepper**
- ▲ **2 medium portobello mushrooms, stems removed, caps thickly sliced**
- **4 slices whole wheat country bread, toasted**
- **4 (¾-ounce) slices light Jarlsberg cheese**

1 Preheat broiler. Line large rimmed baking sheet with foil.

2 Place broccoli and bell pepper on prepared baking sheet. Lightly spray vegetables with olive oil nonstick spray. Sprinkle with garlic, thyme, salt, and black pepper; toss to coat.

3 Broil 4 inches from heat until vegetables begin to char, about 5 minutes. Add mushrooms to vegetable mixture; toss to combine. Continue to broil, tossing twice, until vegetables are tender, about 10 minutes longer.

4 Place bread on second baking sheet; top evenly with vegetable mixture. Top each with a slice of Jarlsberg. Broil until cheese melts, about 1 minute.

Per serving (1 open-face sandwich): 193 Cal, 4 g Total Fat, 2 g Sat Fat, 0 g Trans Fat, 8 mg Chol, 469 mg Sod, 25 g Carb, 8 g Sugar, 5 g Fib, 14 g Prot, 226 mg Calc.

FYI Jarlsberg is a mild creamy cheese from Norway. You can substitute Gruyère, Swiss, or Emmentaler in this recipe.

**VEGAN BURGERS WITH
PINEAPPLE SALSA**

vegan burgers with pineapple salsa

serves 4

2 teaspoons canola oil

4 (2 ½-ounce) meatless vegan burgers

▲ ¼ cup plain fat-free Greek yogurt

1 teaspoon grated lime zest

1 tablespoon lime juice

▲ ½ cup diced fresh pineapple

2 tablespoons chopped fresh mint

▲ 1 cup watercress, trimmed

4 thin whole wheat sandwich rolls, split and toasted

1 Heat oil in large nonstick skillet over medium heat. Add burgers and cook, turning once, until heated through, 6–8 minutes.

2 Meanwhile, stir together yogurt and lime zest and juice in small bowl. Stir together pineapple and mint in second small bowl. Serve burgers and watercress in rolls topped with yogurt sauce and pineapple salsa.

Per serving (1 burger): 260 Cal, 7 g Total Fat, 1 g Sat Fat, 0 g Trans Fat, 0 mg Chol, 626 mg Sod, 39 g Carb, 7 g Sugar, 7 g Fib, 17 g Prot, 114 mg Calc.

roasted corn and avocado quesadillas

serves 4

▲ ½ cup fresh corn kernels (from 1 large ear)

1 teaspoon olive oil

1 ripe avocado, pitted, peeled, and sliced

▲ 1 large tomato, chopped

2 tablespoons chopped fresh cilantro

2 tablespoons toasted shelled pumpkin seeds (pepitas)

4 (8-inch) fat-free whole wheat tortillas

½ cup shredded reduced-fat Monterey Jack cheese

Lime wedges

1 Preheat oven to 375°F. Spray small baking pan with nonstick spray.

2 Place corn in prepared pan. Drizzle with oil and toss to coat. Roast, stirring once, until corn is lightly browned, 10–12 minutes. Transfer to medium bowl and let cool.

3 Add avocado, tomato, cilantro, and pumpkin seeds to bowl; toss to combine.

4 Sprinkle each of 2 tortillas with 2 tablespoons Monterey Jack cheese; top evenly with corn mixture. Sprinkle evenly with remaining cheese. Cover with remaining 2 tortillas, pressing down lightly.

5 Lightly spray quesadillas with nonstick spray. Cook, one at a time, in large nonstick skillet over medium heat, until crisp and heated through, about 3 minutes on each side. Cut each quesadilla into 4 wedges. Serve with lime wedges.

Per serving (2 wedges): 290 Cal, 13 g Total Fat, 3 g Sat Fat, 0 g Trans Fat, 9 mg Chol, 329 mg Sod, 38 g Carb, 3 g Sugar, 8 g Fib, 11 g Prot, 172 mg Calc.

fontina and tomato panini

serves 4   ready in 20 minutes or less

4 small whole wheat ciabatta rolls

1 tablespoon red-wine vinegar

2 teaspoons extra-virgin olive oil

▲ **1 cup firmly packed baby arugula**

▲ **2 medium tomatoes, sliced**

4 green olives, pitted and chopped

1 teaspoon capers, drained and minced

½ cup shredded fontina cheese

1 With serrated knife, cut each roll in half, making bottom slightly thicker than top. Use your fingers to pull out and discard some of soft interior of rolls.

2 Whisk together vinegar and oil in small bowl. Brush cut sides of rolls with vinegar mixture. Layer bottom of each roll with arugula, tomatoes, olives, capers, and fontina cheese. Cover with tops.

3 Spray ridged grill pan with nonstick spray and set over medium-high heat. Place sandwiches in pan and top with another heavy skillet to weight them. Cook until cheese is melted and rolls are golden brown and crispy, about 2 minutes on each side (or grill sandwiches in panini press).

Per serving (1 sandwich): 196 Cal, 9 g Total Fat, 3 g Sat Fat, 0 g Trans Fat, 16 mg Chol, 388 mg Sod, 21 g Carb, 6 g Sugar, 4 g Fib, 10 g Prot, 136 mg Calc.

| **CAN'T COMMIT?** Add 2 slices of prosciutto to each sandwich before grilling. One ounce of prosciutto added to a sandwich will increase the per-serving *PointsPlus* value by *3*.

goat cheese, pear, and fig sandwiches

serves 4   ready in 20 minutes or less

3 ounces reduced-fat goat cheese

8 slices whole wheat bread, toasted

2 tablespoons chopped walnuts, toasted

▲ **1 large ripe Bartlett pear, peeled, cored and thinly sliced**

⅛ teaspoon black pepper

3 tablespoons fig preserves

1 Spread goat cheese evenly on 4 slices of bread. Sprinkle walnuts evenly over goat cheese; top with pear slices. Sprinkle pear with pepper.

2 Spread fig preserves evenly on remaining 4 slices of bread; place on top of pear slices. Cut each sandwich in half.

Per serving (1 sandwich): 293 Cal, 9 g Total Fat, 4 g Sat Fat, 1 g Trans Fat, 10 mg Chol, 351 mg Sod, 43 g Carb, 21 g Sugar, 6 g Fib, 12 g Prot, 102 mg Calc.

❙ **FYI** If you can't find fig preserves, you can use apricot preserves in this recipe.

GOAT CHEESE, PEAR, AND
FIG SANDWICHES AND ROMAN-STYLE
VEGETABLE AND BEAN SOUP, PAGE 44

herbed cheese, beet, and arugula sandwiches

serves 4

▲ ¾ **pound small beets, trimmed**

¼ **cup light garlic and herb cheese spread**

8 **slices whole wheat bread**

▲ ½ **cup firmly packed baby arugula**

1 Preheat oven to 425°F. Place beets on center of double layer of foil; fold edges together to seal tightly. Place packet on baking sheet and roast until beets are fork-tender, about 40 minutes. Unwrap beets and let cool. Peel beets and cut into thin slices.

2 Spread 1 tablespoon herb cheese on each of 4 slices of bread. Top evenly with arugula and beets. Cover with remaining bread slices; cut sandwiches in half.

Per serving (1 sandwich): 190 Cal, 4 g Total Fat, 2 g Sat Fat, 0 g Trans Fat, 7 mg Chol, 343 mg Sod, 30 g Carb, 10 g Sugar, 5 g Fib, 9 g Prot, 84 mg Calc.

FYI To save time, you can make these sandwiches with vacuum-packed precooked beets. Look for them in large supermarkets. Or, you can use canned beets.

grilled vegetable wraps with provolone

serves 4

- ▲ **4 plum tomatoes, halved**
- ▲ **2 zucchini, quartered lengthwise**
- ▲ **1 red onion, cut into ¼-inch slices**
- **¼ cup firmly packed chopped fresh basil**
- **1 tablespoon balsamic vinegar**
- **¼ teaspoon salt**
- **¼ teaspoon black pepper**
- **4 (2-ounce) low-fat whole wheat flatbreads**
- **4 (¾-ounce) slices reduced-fat provolone cheese**

1 Spray grill rack with nonstick spray. Preheat grill to medium-high or prepare medium-hot fire.

2 Lightly spray tomatoes, zucchini, and onion with olive oil nonstick spray. Place vegetables on grill rack. Grill, turning occasionally, until lightly charred and softened, about 5 minutes for tomatoes and about 10 minutes for zucchini and onion.

3 Transfer vegetables to cutting board; coarsely chop. Transfer to medium bowl. Stir in basil, vinegar, salt, and pepper.

4 Lay flatbreads on work surface. Top each with 1 slice provolone cheese; then with grilled vegetable mixture. Roll up flatbreads jelly-roll style.

Per serving (1 wrap): 251 Cal, 6 g Total Fat, 3 g Sat Fat, 0 g Trans Fat, 12 mg Chol, 648 mg Sod, 40 g Carb, 10 g Sugar, 6 g Fib, 13 g Prot, 203 mg Calc.

MANCHEGO AND AVOCADO WRAPS

manchego and avocado wraps

serves 4   ready in 20 minutes or less

¼ cup lime juice

1½ tablespoons extra-virgin olive oil

2 teaspoons sugar

⅛ teaspoon salt

3–4 drops hot sauce

▲ 2 cups shredded green cabbage

▲ 2 cups shredded red cabbage

▲ 1 cup shredded carrots

½ cup chopped fresh cilantro

4 (8-inch) fat-free whole wheat tortillas

1 avocado, pitted, peeled, and cut into ½-inch pieces

▲ 1 medium tomato, diced

¼ cup shredded manchego cheese

1 Whisk together lime juice, olive oil, sugar, salt, and hot sauce in large bowl. Add green cabbage, red cabbage, carrots, and cilantro; toss to coat. Let stand 10 minutes.

2 Place tortillas on work surface. Divide cabbage mixture evenly among 4 tortillas. Top evenly with avocado, tomato, and manchego cheese. Roll up tortillas jelly-roll style.

8 PointsPlus© value

Per serving (1 wrap): 310 Cal, 13 g Total Fat, 3 g Sat Fat, 0 g Trans Fat, 7 mg Chol, 436 mg Sod, 43 g Carb, 8 g Sugar, 9 g Fib, 10 g Prot, 186 mg Calc.

FYI Manchego is a sweet, nutty cheese used in sandwiches and quesadillas. If you prefer, you can use Monterey Jack, Cheddar, or mozzarella in these sandwiches instead.

cucumber and carrot sushi rolls

serves 4

1 cup short-grain white rice

1¼ cups water

1½ tablespoons seasoned rice vinegar

2 teaspoons honey

⅛ teaspoon salt

4 (8 x 7-inch) sheets nori

½–¾ teaspoon wasabi paste

8 teaspoons light cream cheese (Neufchâtel)

▲ 1 large carrot, cut into 16 strips with vegetable peeler

▲ 1 English (seedless) cucumber, peeled, seeded, and cut into 16 strips with vegetable peeler

4 tablespoons reduced-sodium soy sauce

1 tablespoon pickled ginger, thinly sliced

1 Combine rice and water in medium saucepan; bring to boil. Reduce heat and simmer, covered, until the liquid evaporates, about 20 minutes. Remove pan from heat and let stand 10 minutes.

2 Meanwhile, combine vinegar, honey, and salt in small bowl. Stir vinegar mixture into rice until blended; let cool 10 minutes.

3 Place bamboo rolling mat on work surface so that slats are horizontal. Place 1 nori sheet, shiny-side down, with one short side facing you, on mat. Dampen hands with water and spread slightly rounded ½ cup of rice on sheet leaving 1-inch border across the top. Spread ⅛ teaspoon of wasabi crosswise along center of rice. Spread 2 teaspoons cream cheese on top of wasabi. Top wasabi and cream cheese with 4 strips of carrot, then 4 strips of cucumber.

4 Holding filling in place with your fingers, gently roll mat forward with your thumbs until 2 edges of nori overlap to form 7-inch roll. Seal roll with few drops of water on far edge of nori.

5 Transfer roll to cutting board. With sharp knife moistened with water, cut roll crosswise into 6 pieces. Repeat with remaining nori, rice, wasabi, cream cheese, carrot, and cucumber to make 4 rolls. Serve with soy sauce and ginger.

Per serving (6 pieces sushi with 1 tablespoon soy sauce): 244 Cal, 3 g Total Fat, 1 g Sat Fat, 0 g Trans Fat, 7 mg Chol, 767 mg Sod, 48 g Carb, 8 g Sugar, 3 g Fib, 6 g Prot, 56 mg Calc.

tostadas with pickled onions

serves 4

- ▲ ½ small red onion, thinly sliced
- ½ cup apple cider vinegar
- 8 (6-inch) corn tortillas
- ▲ 2 (15½-ounce) cans black beans, drained and rinsed
- ¼ cup lime juice
- 2 garlic cloves, minced
- 2 teaspoons ground cumin
- 2 teaspoons canola oil
- ▲ 2 cups thinly sliced romaine lettuce
- ¼ cup chopped fresh cilantro
- ▲ 1 cup fat-free salsa

1 Combine onion and vinegar in shallow dish. Cover and refrigerate at least 15 minutes and up to 1 week.

2 Preheat oven to 400°F. Line 2 large baking sheets with foil. Lightly spray tortillas on both sides with nonstick spray. Arrange tortillas in single layer on baking sheets. Bake until crisp, about 5 minutes. Set aside.

3 Meanwhile, combine black beans, lime juice, garlic, cumin, and oil in medium microwavable bowl. Coarsely mash bean mixture with potato masher or fork. Cover with wax paper and microwave on High, stirring once, until heated through, 2 minutes.

4 Drain onions; discard vinegar. Spread bean mixture evenly on tortillas. Evenly divide onions, lettuce, and cilantro among tortillas. Serve with salsa.

Per serving (2 tostadas and ¼ cup salsa): 372 Cal, 6 g Total Fat, 1 g Sat Fat, 0 g Trans Fat, 0 mg Chol, 959 mg Sod, 67 g Carb, 4 g Sugar, 20 g Fib, 17 g Prot, 183 mg Calc.

summer rolls with chili-garlic dipping sauce

serves 4

2 tablespoons lime juice

2 teaspoons plus 1 tablespoon reduced-sodium soy sauce

2 teaspoons mirin

▲ 3 cups torn romaine lettuce

▲ 2 carrots, cut into strips

▲ 1 cup thinly sliced yellow bell pepper

▲ ½ English cucumber, halved lengthwise and sliced

2 tablespoons chili-garlic paste

1 tablespoon water

8 rice paper wrappers

▲ 8 ounces firm tofu, drained and cut into ½-inch cubes

½ cup fresh mint leaves

½ cup fresh cilantro leaves

▲ ½ cup salad sprouts or bean sprouts

1 Stir together lime juice, 2 teaspoons soy sauce, and mirin in large bowl. Add lettuce, carrots, bell pepper, and cucumber; toss to coat.

2 To make dipping sauce, stir together chili-garlic paste, remaining 1 tablespoon soy sauce, and water in small bowl. Set aside.

3 To assemble rolls, working one at a time, dip rice wrapper in bowl of warm water. Let stand just until soft, about 30 seconds. Place on clean kitchen towel. Place one-eighth of lettuce mixture, tofu, mint, cilantro, and salad sprouts on rice paper. Fold in sides, then roll up to completely enclose filling. Gently press to seal. Cut each roll diagonally in half. Serve with dipping sauce.

Per serving (2 rolls with 1 tablespoon sauce): 166 Cal, 3 g Total Fat, 0 g Sat Fat, 0 g Trans Fat, 0 mg Chol, 710 mg Sod, 24 g Carb, 5 g Sugar, 3 g Fib, 9 g Prot, 104 mg Calc.

SUMMER ROLLS WITH CHILI-GARLIC
DIPPING SAUCE

spinach
and tomato
pita
pizzas

serves 4

1 teaspoon olive oil

▲ 1 small red onion, chopped

3 garlic cloves, minced

¼ teaspoon salt

▲ 1 (10-ounce) package frozen chopped spinach, thawed and squeezed dry

⅓ cup crumbled reduced-fat feta cheese

2 teaspoons minced fresh dill or 1 teaspoon dried

4 (6-inch) whole-wheat pita breads

▲ 1 cup cherry tomatoes, halved

¾ cup shredded part-skim mozzarella cheese

1 Preheat oven to 425°F.

2 Heat oil in large nonstick skillet over medium heat. Add onion and cook, stirring frequently, until softened, about 4 minutes. Stir in garlic and salt; cook, stirring, about 1 minute. Stir in spinach and cook until hot, about 2 minutes. Remove skillet from heat and stir in feta cheese and dill.

3 Arrange pitas on baking sheet. Top with spinach mixture, spreading to edges. Arrange tomatoes on top. Bake until pitas are crisp, 8–10 minutes.

4 Sprinkle pizzas with mozzarella cheese; bake until melted, about 3 minutes.

Per serving (1 pizza): 280 Cal, 9 g Total Fat, 4 g Sat Fat, 0 g Trans Fat, 18 mg Chol, 777 mg Sod, 38 g Carb, 7 g Sugar, 7 g Fib, 16 g Prot, 277 mg Calc.

southwestern veggie tortilla pizzas

serves 4

4 (7-inch) whole-wheat tortillas

1 teaspoon canola oil

▲ 1 cup fresh corn kernels or frozen corn kernels, thawed

▲ ½ large bell pepper, seeded and cut into 2-inch-long strips

▲ ¼ cup chopped onion

▲ 1 jalapeño pepper, seeded and diced

¾ teaspoon ground cumin

¼ teaspoon salt

1 teaspoon minced chipotle en adobo

▲ 2 plum tomatoes, chopped

¾ cup shredded reduced-fat Monterey Jack cheese

1 Preheat oven to 350°F. Spray large baking sheet with nonstick spray. Place tortillas in single layer in pan and bake until tortillas are crisp, about 10 minutes. Maintain oven temperature.

2 Meanwhile, heat oil in medium nonstick skillet over medium heat. Add corn, bell pepper, onion, jalapeño, cumin, and salt. Cook, stirring occasionally, until vegetables are crisp-tender, about 4 minutes. Remove from heat and stir in chipotle.

3 Spoon vegetable mixture evenly over tortillas; top with tomatoes. Sprinkle with cheese.

4 Return tortillas to oven and bake until cheese melts, about 4 minutes.

Per serving (1 pizza): 189 Cal, 7 g Total Fat, 3 g Sat Fat, 0 g Trans Fat, 14 mg Chol, 421 mg Sod, 24 g Carb, 4 g Sugar, 4 g Fib, 9 g Prot, 168 mg Calc.

**GRILLED ASPARAGUS AND
RICOTTA PIZZA**

grilled asparagus and ricotta pizza

serves 4

3 teaspoons olive oil

1 cup part-skim ricotta

¼ cup chopped fresh mint

2 garlic cloves, minced

Grated zest and juice of 1 lemon

▲ **¾ pound asparagus, trimmed**

1 (1-pound) package store-bought pizza dough

1 Brush grill rack with 1 teaspoon oil. Preheat grill to medium-high or prepare medium-hot fire.

2 Stir together ricotta, mint, garlic, and lemon juice in small bowl; set aside.

3 Combine asparagus and remaining 2 teaspoons oil in large bowl; toss to coat. Place asparagus on grill rack. Grill, turning often, until asparagus is crisp-tender, about 3 minutes. Transfer asparagus to large clean bowl. Add lemon zest and toss to coat.

4 On lightly floured surface, roll dough into 9 x 12-inch rectangle. Lightly spray dough with olive oil cooking spray on both sides. Place dough on grill rack and grill until browned on underside, about 3 minutes. Remove crust from grill.

5 Spread ricotta mixture evenly over browned side of crust. Arrange asparagus on top of ricotta. Return pizza to grill rack and grill until underside is browned, about 3 minutes.

Per serving (¼ of pizza): 418 Cal, 15 g Total Fat, 5 g Sat Fat, 0 g Trans Fat, 19 mg Chol, 554 mg Sod, 56 g Carb, 3 g Sugar, 4 g Fib, 15 g Prot, 199 mg Calc.

CAN'T COMMIT? Add ½ pound large shrimp, peeled and deveined to the asparagus mixture in step 3. Proceed with the recipe, grilling the shrimp until just opaque in the center, about 3 minutes. Add the shrimp to the pizza when you add the asparagus in step 5. The per-serving *PointsPlus* value will increase by *2*.

roman-style vegetable and bean soup

serves 4

▲ 2 teaspoons olive oil
▲ 1 onion, chopped
▲ 1 stalk celery, chopped
  3 garlic cloves, minced
▲ 4 cups reduced-sodium vegetable broth
▲ 1 (15-ounce) can diced tomatoes
▲ 2 carrots, chopped
▲ 1 (15-ounce) can cannellini (white kidney) beans
  1 teaspoon dried oregano
  1 teaspoon dried basil
  ½ teaspoon red pepper flakes
  ⅛ teaspoon salt
▲ 2 large zucchini, chopped
  ¼ cup chopped fresh flat-leaf parsley

1 Heat oil in large heavy-bottomed saucepan over medium-high heat. Add onion, celery, and garlic and cook, stirring occasionally, until softened, 5 minutes.

2 Add broth, tomatoes, carrots, beans, oregano, basil, pepper flakes, and salt to saucepan. Bring to boil. Reduce heat and cover. Simmer until vegetables are almost tender, about 10 minutes.

3 Add zucchini and simmer until zucchini is crisp-tender, 5 minutes. Ladle soup into 4 bowls; sprinkle with parsley.

Per serving (about 2 cups): 201 Cal, 3 g Total Fat, 1 g Sat Fat, 0 g Trans Fat, 0 mg Chol, 864 mg Sod, 36 g Carb, 13 g Sugar, 9 g Fib, 10 g Prot, 128 mg Calc.

STAY ON TRACK Get more veggies in your diet and add 1 (10-ounce) package frozen thawed artichoke hearts, quartered, when you add the zucchini in step 3.

curried red lentil and apple soup

serves 4

- 2 Granny Smith apples
- 1 tablespoon canola oil
- 1 medium sweet onion, chopped
- 2 carrots, chopped
- 3 garlic cloves, minced
- 1 tablespoon mild curry powder
- 3 cups water
- 1 (14½-ounce) can reduced-sodium vegetable broth
- ½ pound (1¼ cups) red lentils, picked over and rinsed
- 4 tablespoons plain fat-free Greek yogurt

1 Peel, halve, core, and chop one apple. Heat oil in large saucepan over medium-high heat. Add chopped apple, onion, carrots, and garlic. Cook, stirring often, until softened, 5 minutes. Add curry and cook, stirring constantly, until fragrant, 30 seconds.

2 Add water, broth, and lentils; bring to boil. Reduce heat and cover. Simmer until lentils are tender, 30 minutes. Let cool 5 minutes.

3 Pour soup, in batches, into blender; puree. Return soup to saucepan. Reheat over medium heat.

4 Halve, core, and thinly slice remaining apple. Ladle soup into 4 bowls. Top evenly with apple slices and yogurt.

Per serving (1½ cups soup, ¼ apple, and 1 tablespoon yogurt): 292 Cal, 4 g Total Fat, 0 g Sat Fat, 0 g Trans Fat, 0 mg Chol, 236 mg Sod, 50 g Carb, 13 g Sugar, 12 g Fib, 17 g Prot, 87 mg Calc.

❚ FYI If you prefer a chunky soup, skip step 3 (pureeing the soup).

barley soup with fennel and zucchini

serves 4

1 cup water

▲ ½ cup quick-cooking barley

1 tablespoon extra-virgin olive oil

▲ 2 carrots, chopped

▲ 1 fennel bulb, trimmed and coarsely chopped

▲ 1 celery stalk, thinly sliced

3 garlic cloves, minced

1 tablespoon chopped fresh tarragon or 1 teaspoon dried

▲ 1 (32-ounce) container reduced-sodium vegetable broth

▲ 1 zucchini, halved lengthwise and thinly sliced

1 Bring water to boil in medium saucepan over high heat; add barley. Reduce heat, cover, and simmer until tender, about 10 minutes.

2 Meanwhile, heat oil in large saucepan over medium-high heat. Add carrots, fennel, and celery. Cook, stirring often, until vegetables are softened, 5 minutes. Add garlic and tarragon; cook, stirring constantly, until fragrant, 1 minute

3 Add broth; bring to boil. Reduce heat and add zucchini. Cover and simmer until vegetables are tender, 10 minutes. Stir in barley and cook until heated through, about 2 minutes.

Per serving (1¾ cups): 150 Cal, 4 g Total Fat, 1 g Sat Fat, 0 g Trans Fat, 0 mg Chol, 499 mg Sod, 27 g Carb, 9 g Sugar, 6 g Fib, 4 g Prot, 72 mg Calc.

| **FYI** If you don't like the flavor of tarragon, you can substitute thyme or oregano in this recipe.

fresh corn soup with basil

serves 4

- **1 tablespoon canola oil**
- ▲ **1 sweet onion, chopped**
- ▲ **6 ears corn on the cob, kernels removed**
- **3 garlic cloves, chopped**
- ▲ **1 (32-ounce) container reduced-sodium vegetable broth**
- **⅛ teaspoon salt**
- **Thinly sliced fresh basil leaves**

1 Heat oil in large saucepan over medium-high heat. Add onion and cook, stirring often, until softened, 5 minutes. Add corn and garlic. Cook, stirring often, until corn is softened, 5 minutes. Stir in vegetable broth and salt; bring to boil. Reduce heat and simmer 10 minutes. Let stand 5 minutes.

2 Transfer 3 cups soup to blender and puree. Return to saucepan and cook over low heat until hot, 2 minutes. Ladle into 4 bowls; sprinkle evenly with basil.

Per serving (1½ cups): 207 Cal, 6 g Total Fat, 1 g Sat Fat, 0 g Trans Fat, 0 mg Chol, 508 mg Sod, 40 g Carb, 16 g Sugar, 5 g Fib, 6 g Prot, 21 mg Calc.

CAN'T COMMIT? Top each bowl of soup with a slice of crumbled crisp-cooked bacon. One bacon slice per serving will increase the **PointsPlus** value by **1**.

potato and celery root soup with blue cheese

serves 6

2 teaspoons canola oil

▲ 1 small onion, chopped

3 garlic cloves, minced

▲ 2 russet potatoes (1¼ pounds), peeled and diced

▲ 1 small celery root (1 pound), peeled and diced

▲ 1 (14½-ounce) can reduced-sodium vegetable broth

1½ cups water

⅛ teaspoon salt

¼ teaspoon black pepper

¾ cup low-fat (1%) milk

¼ teaspoon ground nutmeg

¼ cup crumbled reduced-fat blue cheese

Chopped fresh chives

1 Heat oil in large saucepan over medium-high heat. Add onion and cook, stirring often, until softened, 5 minutes. Add garlic and cook, stirring constantly, until fragrant, 30 seconds.

2 Add potatoes, celery root, broth, water, salt, and pepper. Bring to boil. Reduce heat and cover. Simmer until vegetables are tender, about 15 minutes. Let cool 5 minutes.

3 Puree soup, in batches if necessary, in blender. Return soup to saucepan; set over medium heat. Stir in milk and nutmeg. Cook, stirring occasionally, until soup is heated through, 3 minutes. Ladle soup into 6 bowls. Sprinkle 2 teaspoons blue cheese on each serving and garnish with chives.

Per serving (1 cup soup and 2 teaspoons blue cheese): 145 Cal, 3 g Total Fat, 1 g Sat Fat, 0 g Trans Fat, 10 mg Chol, 308 mg Sod, 26 g Carb, 7 g Sugar, 3 g Fib, 5 g Prot, 100 mg Calc.

gingery sweet potato and carrot soup

serves 4

2 teaspoons olive oil

▲ 1 small onion, chopped

2 tablespoons minced peeled fresh ginger

▲ 3 carrots, chopped

▲ 2 sweet potatoes (1¼ pounds), peeled and chopped

▲ 1 (32-ounce) container reduced-sodium vegetable broth

1 tablespoon lemon juice

1 Heat oil in large saucepan over medium-high heat. Add onion and cook, stirring occasionally, until softened, 5 minutes. Add ginger and cook, stirring constantly, until fragrant, 1 minute.

2 Stir in carrots, sweet potatoes, and broth. Bring to boil. Reduce heat and cover. Simmer until vegetables are tender, about 20 minutes. Let cool 5 minutes.

3 Puree soup, in batches if necessary, in blender. Return soup to saucepan; set over medium heat. Stir in lemon juice. Cook, stirring occasionally, until soup is heated through, 3 minutes.

Per serving (1 cup): 120 Cal, 3 g Total Fat, 0 g Sat Fat, 0 g Trans Fat, 0 mg Chol, 478 mg Sod, 24 g Carb, 10 g Sugar, 4 g Fib, 2 g Prot, 45 mg Calc.

**THAI COCONUT AND VEGETABLE
NOODLE SOUP**

thai coconut and vegetable noodle soup

serves 6

- 3 ounces 100% buckwheat (soba) noodles
- 2 teaspoons canola oil
- 3 garlic cloves, minced
- 1 tablespoon grated peeled fresh ginger
- 1 (32-ounce) container reduced-sodium vegetable broth
- 1 small red bell pepper, diced
- 2 carrots, cut into thin strips
- ¼ pound sugar snap peas, trimmed and cut in half
- ⅓ cup light (reduced-fat) coconut milk
- ¼ cup fresh cilantro leaves
- ¼ cup dry roasted unsalted peanuts, chopped
- Lime wedges

1 Cook noodles according to package directions.

2 Meanwhile, heat oil in large saucepan over medium-high heat. Add garlic and ginger. Cook, stirring constantly, until fragrant, 1 minute. Stir in broth, bell pepper, and carrots. Bring to boil. Reduce heat and cover. Simmer, until vegetables are softened, 5 minutes. Add sugar snap peas. Cover and cook until vegetables are crisp tender, 5 minutes longer.

3 Add noodles and coconut milk; cook until heated through, 2 minutes. Stir in cilantro. Ladle soup into 6 bowls. Sprinkle evenly with peanuts and serve with lime wedges.

Per serving (1 cup soup and 2 teaspoons peanuts): 131 Cal, 5 g Total Fat, 1 g Sat Fat, 0 g Trans Fat, 0 mg Chol, 363 mg Sod, 18 g Carb, 5 g Sugar, 4 g Fib, 5 g Prot, 30 mg Calc.

sweet potato and bean chili

serves 6

1 tablespoon canola oil

▲ 1 onion, chopped

▲ 2 carrots, sliced

1 chipotle en adobo, chopped

1 tablespoon ground cumin

▲ 2 sweet potatoes (1 pound), peeled and cut into 1-inch pieces

▲ 1 (28-ounce) can crushed tomatoes

▲ 1 (14½-ounce) can reduced-sodium vegetable broth

▲ 1 (15-ounce) can red kidney beans, rinsed and drained

▲ 1 (15-ounce) can black beans, rinsed and drained

▲ 4 tablespoons plain fat-free Greek yogurt

Chopped fresh cilantro

1 Heat oil in large saucepan over medium-high heat. Add onion and carrots. Cook, stirring occasionally, until softened, 5 minutes. Add chipotle and cumin; cook, stirring constantly, 1 minute.

2 Add sweet potatoes, tomatoes, broth, kidney beans, and black beans; bring to boil. Reduce heat, cover, and simmer until sweet potatoes are tender, 20–25 minutes.

3 Ladle chili into 6 bowls. Top each portion with 2 teaspoons yogurt and sprinkle with cilantro.

Per serving (1⅓ cups soup and 1 tablespoon yogurt): 251 Cal, 3 g Total Fat, 0 g Sat Fat, 0 g Trans Fat, 0 mg Chol, 888 mg Sod, 46 g Carb, 12 g Sugar, 13 g Fib, 12 g Prot, 131 mg Calc.

CAN'T COMMIT? Cook 8 ounces ground skinless chicken breast with the onions and carrots in step 1. The per-serving *PointsPlus* value will increase by *1*.

mango and cucumber gazpacho

serves 4

- ▲ **3 large mangoes, peeled, pitted, and chopped**
- ▲ **2 cucumbers, peeled, seeded, and chopped**
- ▲ **1 yellow bell pepper, chopped**
- **1½ cups low-fat buttermilk**
- **1 garlic clove, chopped**
- **1 tablespoon lime juice**
- **1 teaspoon seasoned rice vinegar**
- **1–2 drops hot sauce (optional)**

1 Set aside ½ cup each chopped mango and chopped cucumber.

2 Place remaining mangoes, remaining cucumbers, bell pepper, 1 cup buttermilk, and garlic in blender. Puree until smooth. Add remaining ½ cup buttermilk, lime juice, vinegar, and hot sauce (if using); pulse until blended.

3 Transfer to medium bowl. Stir in reserved mango and cucumber. Cover and refrigerate until chilled, at least 2 hours or up to 3 days.

Per serving (1 cup): 227 Cal, 2 g Total Fat, 1 g Sat Fat, 0 g Trans Fat, 4 mg Chol, 122 mg Sod, 51 g Carb, 45 g Sugar, 5 g Fib, 6 g Prot, 156 mg Calc.

smoky three-cheese mac' and cheese

serves 8

- ▲ **1 pound whole wheat penne or cavatappi**
- ▲ **3 cups fat-free milk**
- **3 tablespoons all-purpose flour**
- **4 ounces reduced-fat cream cheese, cut into cubes**
- **1 cup shredded reduced-fat Cheddar**
- **1 cup shredded smoked mozzarella**
- **1 teaspoon smoked paprika**
- **½ teaspoon salt**
- **1 cup panko bread crumbs**

1 Cook cavatappi according to package directions, omitting salt if desired.

2 Preheat broiler. Spray 4-quart flameproof casserole dish with nonstick spray.

3 Meanwhile, whisk together milk and flour in large saucepan until smooth. Set over medium-high heat and cook, whisking constantly, until mixture comes to boil and thickens, about 4 minutes. Remove from heat. Add cream cheese, Cheddar, mozzarella, paprika, and salt. Whisk until smooth. Stir in pasta.

4 Transfer mixture to prepared casserole dish. Sprinkle evenly with crumbs; spray crumbs lightly with nonstick spray. Broil until crumbs are lightly browned, 2–3 minutes.

Per serving (2 cups): 377 Cal, 9 g Total Fat, 5 g Sat Fat, 0 g Trans Fat, 28 mg Chol, 669 mg Sod, 56 g Carb, 7 g Sugar, 5 g Fib, 21 g Prot, 352 mg Calc.

**SMOKY THREE-CHEESE
MAC' AND CHEESE**

chilled strawberry and ginger beet soup

serves 6

▲ **3 medium beets, peeled and chopped (1 pound)**

▲ **½ medium Yukon Gold potato, peeled and chopped**

3 cups water

½ teaspoon salt

▲ **2 cups fresh or thawed frozen sliced strawberries**

1 tablespoon grated peeled fresh ginger

1½ tablespoons lime juice

2 teaspoons honey

6 tablespoons plain low-fat yogurt

1 Combine beets, potato, water, and salt in large saucepan; bring to boil. Reduce heat and simmer, covered, until beets are very tender, 45 minutes. Let cool about 10 minutes.

2 Pour soup, in batches, into blender and puree, adding strawberries and ginger to one batch. Press puree through a strainer; discard solids. Stir in lime juice and honey.

3 Cover and refrigerate until chilled, at least 3 hours or up to 8 hours. Ladle soup into 6 bowls and top with yogurt.

Per serving (about ¾ cup soup with 1 tablespoon yogurt): 68 Cal, 1 g Total Fat, 0 g Sat Fat, 0 g Trans Fat, 1 mg Chol, 244 mg Sod, 15 g Carb, 9 g Sugar, 3 g Fib, 2 g Prot, 48 mg Calc.

FYI Serve this soup with a sandwich or salad to make a filling lunch. Try Grilled Vegetable Wraps with Provolone, page 33 or Sweet Potato, Pecan, and Goat Cheese Salad, page 66.

tropical tofu salad

serves 4

2 teaspoons canola oil

▲ 1 (14-ounce) package firm tofu, drained and cut into ½-inch cubes

¼ cup lime juice

1 teaspoon ground cumin

2 garlic cloves, minced

¾ teaspoon salt

▲ 1 mango, peeled, pitted, and diced

▲ 1 English (seedless) cucumber, thinly sliced

▲ 1 (14-ounce) can hearts of palm, drained and thinly sliced

▲ ½ small red onion, minced

½ small avocado, halved, pitted, peeled, and diced

½ cup chopped fresh cilantro

1 Heat oil in large nonstick skillet over medium heat. Add tofu and cook, turning often, until lightly browned, 6–8 minutes. Transfer to plate and let cool.

2 Stir together lime juice, cumin, garlic, and salt in large bowl. Add tofu, mango, cucumber, hearts of palm, onion, avocado, and cilantro; toss to coat. Cover and refrigerate at least 30 minutes or up to 8 hours. Toss before serving.

Per serving (1¼ cups): 212 Cal, 10 g Total Fat, 2 g Sat Fat, 0 g Trans Fat, 0 mg Chol, 777 mg Sod, 25 g Carb, 14 g Sugar, 6 g Fib, 12 g Prot, 279 mg Calc.

BRUSSELS SPROUTS, PEAR,
AND FRICO SALAD

brussels sprouts, pear, and frico salad

serves 4

- 2 (10-ounce) containers Brussels sprouts, trimmed and halved
- ¼ cup shredded Parmesan cheese
- 1 teaspoon grated lemon zest
- 2 tablespoons lemon juice
- 1 tablespoon extra-virgin olive oil
- ⅛ teaspoon salt
- ¼ teaspoon black pepper
- 1 (5-ounce) package baby spinach leaves
- 1 ripe pear, thinly sliced

1 Adjust oven racks to divide oven into thirds and preheat to 425°F. Spray large rimmed baking sheet with nonstick spray.

2 Place Brussels sprouts on prepared baking sheet. Lightly spray with nonstick spray and toss to coat. Arrange Brussels sprouts in single layer. Roast on top oven rack, stirring once, until tender and browned, about 30 minutes.

3 Meanwhile, line second large baking sheet with parchment paper. Place Parmesan by teaspoonfuls, 1 inch apart, on parchment-lined baking sheet, making 12 crisps in total. Bake on bottom oven rack until very lightly browned, about 7 minutes. Let cool on baking sheet about 1 minute. Transfer crisps with spatula to rack and cool completely.

4 To make salad, whisk together lemon zest and juice, oil, salt, and pepper in large bowl. Add Brussels sprouts, spinach, and pear; toss to coat. Divide salad among 4 plates; top each salad with 3 Parmesan crisps.

Per serving (2 cups salad and 3 parmesan crisps): 148 Cal, 7 g Total Fat, 2 g Sat Fat, 0 g Trans Fat, 5 mg Chol, 228 mg Sod, 19 g Carb, 11 g Sugar, 6 g Fib, 7 g Prot, 178 mg Calc.

FYI Frico are Italian cheese crisps made with shredded Parmesan that is simply mounded on a baking sheet and baked until crisp. They add a flavorful finishing touch to soups or salads.

white bean, tomato, and mint salad

serves 4   ready in 20 minutes or less

2 tablespoons lemon juice

1 tablespoon extra-virgin olive oil

¼ teaspoon black pepper

▲ 1 (15-ounce) can cannellini (white kidney) beans, rinsed and drained

▲ 1 pint grape tomatoes, halved

▲ 3 scallions, thinly sliced

2 tablespoons chopped fresh mint

▲ 4 cups mixed salad greens

4 tablespoons reduced-fat crumbled feta cheese

1 Whisk together lemon juice, oil, and pepper in medium bowl. Add beans, tomatoes, scallions, and mint; toss to coat.

2 Divide salad greens among 4 plates. Top evenly with bean mixture and sprinkle 1 tablespoon feta over each salad.

Per serving (1 plate): 185 Cal, 5 g Total Fat, 1 g Sat Fat, 0 g Trans Fat, 5 mg Chol, 357 mg Sod, 26 g Carb, 4 g Sugar, 7 g Fib, 11 g Prot, 136 mg Calc.

STAY ON TRACK Serve warmed whole wheat pita bread with this salad. A small (1-ounce) whole wheat pita for each serving will increase the *PointsPlus* value by *2*.

lentil salad with oranges and olives

serves 4

- 1 cup French green lentils, picked over and rinsed
- 1 teaspoon grated orange zest
- ¼ cup orange juice
- 1 tablespoon extra-virgin olive oil
- 1 teaspoon honey
- 1 teaspoon chopped fresh rosemary
- ⅛ teaspoon salt
- ¼ teaspoon black pepper
- 2 navel oranges, peeled, halved, and cut crosswise into thin slices
- 1 small red onion, thinly sliced
- 8 pitted black olives, sliced
- 1 (6-ounce) package baby spinach leaves

1 Place lentils in medium saucepan; add enough water to cover by 2 inches. Bring to boil over high heat. Reduce heat and cover. Simmer until lentils are tender and still hold their shape, 20 minutes. Drain. Transfer to large bowl and let cool to room temperature.

2 Whisk together orange zest and juice, oil, honey, rosemary, salt, and pepper in small bowl. Add to lentils; toss to coat. Add orange slices, onion, olives, and spinach; toss to combine.

Per serving (2¼ cups): 275 Cal, 7 g Total Fat, 1 g Sat Fat, 0 g Trans Fat, 0 mg Chol, 167 mg Sod, 42 g Carb, 10 g Sugar, 11 g Fib, 14 g Prot, 111 mg Calc.

QUINOA AND ROASTED
VEGETABLE SALAD

quinoa and roasted vegetable salad

serves 4

- ▲ **2 zucchini, halved lengthwise and sliced**
- ▲ **2 small yellow squash, halved lengthwise and sliced**
- ▲ **1 red onion, halved and cut into ¼-inch wedges**
- **2 garlic cloves, minced**
- **1 tablespoon plus 2 teaspoons extra-virgin olive oil**
- **1 tablespoon chopped fresh oregano or 1 teaspoon dried**
- **¼ teaspoon salt**
- **¼ teaspoon black pepper**
- **1 cup water**
- ▲ **½ cup quinoa, rinsed**
- **2 tablespoons lemon juice**
- ▲ **3 cups firmly packed baby arugula leaves**

1 Preheat oven to 425°F. Spray large rimmed baking sheet with nonstick spray.

2 Place zucchini, yellow squash, onion, and garlic on prepared baking sheet. Drizzle 1 tablespoon oil over vegetables and sprinkle with oregano, salt, and pepper. Toss to coat. Arrange vegetables in single layer. Roast, turning once, until vegetables are tender and browned, about 20 minutes.

3 Meanwhile, combine water and quinoa in small saucepan; bring to boil. Reduce heat and cover. Simmer until liquid is absorbed and quinoa is tender, about 10 minutes. Drain in fine-mesh sieve. Rinse under cold running water and drain again.

4 Whisk together lemon juice and remaining 2 teaspoons oil in large bowl. Add roasted vegetables, quinoa, and arugula; toss to coat.

Per serving (1⅓ cups): 174 Cal, 8 g Total Fat, 1 g Sat Fat, 0 g Trans Fat, 0 mg Chol, 165 mg Sod, 23 g Carb, 6 g Sugar, 4 g Fib, 6 g Prot, 75 mg Calc.

CAN'T COMMIT? Add 8 ounces shredded skinless cooked chicken breast to the salad. The per-serving *PointsPlus* value will increase by *2*.

barley, butternut, and almond salad

serves 4

- ▲ **1 small butternut squash (2 pounds), peeled, seeded, and cubed**
- **3 shallots, sliced**
- **¼ teaspoon salt**
- ▲ **1 cup quick-cooking barley**
- **2 tablespoons white balsamic vinegar or white-wine vinegar**
- **2 teaspoons olive oil**
- **⅛ teaspoon black pepper**
- **⅓ cup golden raisins**
- **¼ cup chopped toasted almonds**
- **2 tablespoons minced fresh flat-leaf parsley**

1 Preheat oven to 425°F. Spray large rimmed baking sheet with nonstick spray.

2 Place squash and shallots on prepared baking sheet; lightly spray with nonstick spray. Sprinkle vegetables with ⅛ teaspoon salt; toss to coat. Bake, stirring occasionally, until vegetables are lightly browned and tender, 35 minutes.

3 Meanwhile, cook barley according to package directions; drain.

4 Whisk together vinegar, oil, remaining ⅛ teaspoon salt, and pepper in large bowl. Add squash mixture, barley, raisins, almonds, and parsley; toss to coat.

Per serving (1 cup): 321 Cal, 8 g Total Fat, 1 g Sat Fat, 0 g Trans Fat, 0 mg Chol, 164 mg Sod, 61 g Carb, 16 g Sugar, 13 g Fib, 8 g Prot, 118 mg Calc.

STAY ON TRACK Make this salad more filling and nutritious by serving it on a bed of watercress.

heirloom tomato salad with goat cheese

serves 4

- ▲ **2 heirloom tomatoes, thickly sliced**
- ▲ **1 green bell pepper, quartered**
- ▲ **1 yellow bell pepper, quartered**
- **2 tablespoons lemon juice**
- **1 teaspoon olive oil**
- **1 teaspoon chopped fresh oregano or ½ teaspoon dried**
- **1 garlic clove, minced**
- **⅛ teaspoon salt**
- **⅛ teaspoon black pepper**
- ▲ **1 (5-ounce) container baby arugula**
- **4 ounces reduced-fat goat cheese, crumbled**

1 Spray cast-iron ridged grill pan with nonstick spray and set over medium-high heat. Place tomatoes and bell peppers in pan. Grill, turning occasionally, until vegetables are lightly charred, 3–4 minutes for tomatoes and 6–8 minutes for bell peppers. Transfer to plate.

2 To make dressing, whisk together lemon juice, oil, oregano, garlic, salt, and pepper in large bowl. Set aside.

3 Add arugula to bowl; toss to coat. Divide salad among 4 plates. Evenly divide bell peppers and tomatoes among salads. Sprinkle evenly with goat cheese.

Per serving (1 plate): 97 Cal, 5 g Total Fat, 2 g Sat Fat, 0 g Trans Fat, 5 mg Chol, 188 mg Sod, 10 g Carb, 6 g Sugar, 3 g Fib, 6 g Prot, 117 mg Calc.

FYI Heirloom tomatoes, unlike regular supermarket tomatoes, have not been bred to have uniform shape and a long shelf life. Though they look unusual and are highly perishable, their fantastic flavor makes them worth seeking out at farmers' markets.

sweet potato, pecan, and goat cheese salad

serves 4

▲ **2 sweet potatoes (1 pound), peeled and cut into chunks**

1 teaspoon ground cumin

2 tablespoons lemon juice

1 tablespoon extra-virgin olive oil

2 teaspoons Dijon mustard

½ teaspoon honey

¼ teaspoon kosher salt

▲ **4 cups firmly packed baby arugula leaves**

3 tablespoons chopped pecans, toasted

4 tablespoons crumbled reduced-fat goat cheese

1 Preheat oven to 425°F. Spray large rimmed baking sheet with nonstick spray.

2 Place sweet potatoes on prepared baking sheet; lightly spray with nonstick spray. Sprinkle with cumin and toss to coat. Arrange potatoes in single layer. Bake, turning once, until tender and browned, about 30 minutes.

3 Whisk together lemon juice, oil, mustard, honey, and salt in large bowl. Add sweet potatoes, arugula, and pecans; toss to coat. Divide salad among 4 plates; top evenly with goat cheese.

Per serving (1¾ cups salad and 1 tablespoon cheese): 159 Cal, 10 g Total Fat, 2 g Sat Fat, 0 g Trans Fat, 4 mg Chol, 232 mg Sod, 15 g Carb, 5 g Sugar, 3 g Fib, 4 g Prot, 77 mg Calc.

CAN'T COMMIT? Add 6 ounces cubed reduced-sodium lean ham to the salad. The per-serving *PointsPlus* will increase by *1*.

sesame and ginger citrus salad

serves 4

- ▲ **3 navel oranges**
- ▲ **2 pink grapefruits**
- **1 tablespoon olive oil**
- **1 teaspoon balsamic vinegar**
- **1 teaspoon reduced-sodium soy sauce**
- **¼ teaspoon grated fresh peeled ginger**
- **⅛ teaspoon salt**
- ▲ **2 scallions, cut diagonally into thin slices**
- **1 tablespoon toasted sesame seeds**

1 Grate ½ teaspoon zest from 1 orange and place in small bowl. With sharp knife, peel oranges and grapefruits, removing all white pith. Cut oranges and grapefruits into thick rounds and arrange on platter.

2 Add oil, vinegar, soy sauce, ginger, and salt to orange zest; whisk to combine. Drizzle over citrus; sprinkle with scallions and sesame seeds.

Per serving (about 1 cup): 149 Cal, 5 g Total Fat, 1 g Sat Fat, 0 g Trans Fat, 0 mg Chol, 118 mg Sod, 26 g Carb, 18 g Sugar, 5 g Fib, 3 g Prot, 75 mg Calc.

FYI Serve this colorful salad with Thai Coconut and Vegetable Noodle Soup, page 51 or Herbed Cheese, Beet, and Arugula Sandwiches, page 32 for a healthful and filling lunch.

cantaloupe
and
bocconcini
salad

serves 4 ready in 20 minutes or less

1 tablespoon lime juice

2 teaspoons extra-virgin olive oil

2 tablespoons chopped fresh mint

¼ teaspoon salt

¼ teaspoon black pepper

▲ 1 small ripe cantaloupe, halved, seeded, peeled, and cubed

4 ounces bocconcini (small fresh mozzarella balls), halved

▲ 2 cups firmly packed baby arugula leaves

1 Whisk together lime juice, oil, mint, salt, and pepper in large bowl.

2 Add cantalope, bocconcini, and arugula; toss to combine.

Per serving (1 cup): 142 Cal, 10 g Total Fat, 4 g Sat Fat, 0 g Trans Fat, 20 mg Chol, 308 mg Sod, 10 g Carb, 9 g Sugar, 1 g Fib, 7 g Prot, 129 mg Calc.

FYI If you like, you can make this salad using halved cherry tomatoes instead of the cantaloupe. You will need about 2 cups of cherry tomatoes.

CANTALOUPE AND BOCCONCINI SALAD

halloumi, fig, and pomegranate salad

serves 4 ready in 20 minutes or less

¼ cup pomegranate juice

3½ teaspoons olive oil

1 teaspoon Dijon mustard

1 teaspoon grated lemon zest

¼ teaspoon black pepper

▲ 4 fresh figs, halved and sliced

12 thin slices halloumi cheese (about 2 ounces)

▲ 1 (6-ounce) bag baby spinach leaves

2 tablespoons chopped pecans, toasted

1 Whisk together pomegranate juice, 2 teaspoons oil, mustard, lemon zest, and pepper in large bowl. Add figs and toss to coat. Set aside.

2 Coat large nonstick skillet with ½ teaspoon remaining oil; set over medium heat. Add 4 slices halloumi. Cook, turning once, until lightly browned, about 2 minutes. Transfer cheese to large platter and keep warm. Repeat with remaining oil and cheese.

3 Add spinach and pecans to fig mixture; toss to coat. Divide salad among 4 plates; top each with 3 slices of cheese.

Per serving (2½ cups salad and 3 halloumi slices): 149 Cal, 9 g Total Fat, 3 g Sat Fat, 0 g Trans Fat, 10 mg Chol, 198 mg Sod, 14 g Carb, 6 g Sugar, 3 g Fib, 5 g Prot, 196 mg Calc.

FYI Halloumi is a semihard cheese with a high melting temperature, so you can cook it in a skillet and brown the slices before they begin to melt. If you can't find it, you can substitute your favorite cheese, omitting step 2 of the recipe.

shaved kale salad with pecorino romano

serves 4 ready in 20 minutes or less

2 tablespoons lemon juice

2 teaspoons extra-virgin olive oil

¼ teaspoon salt

⅛ teaspoon black pepper

▲ 2 bunches lacinato kale, ribs discarded and thinly sliced

¼ cup shaved pecorino Romano

1 Whisk together lemon juice, oil, salt, and pepper. Add kale and toss to coat. Let stand at room temperature, tossing occasionally, 10 minutes.

2 Divide kale mixture among 4 plates. Top with pecorino.

Per serving (2 cups): 101 Cal, 5 g Total Fat, 2 g Sat Fat, 0 g Trans Fat, 7 mg Chol, 277 mg Sod, 11 g Carb, 2 g Sugar, 2 g Fib, 6 g Prot, 216 mg Calc.

| **CAN'T COMMIT?** Top each salad with 1 ounce prosciutto cut into thin strips. The per-serving *PointsPlus* value will increase by *3*.

"california roll" salad

serves 4

▲ **1 cup short-grain brown rice**

¼ cup rice vinegar

3 tablespoons reduced-sodium soy sauce

2 teaspoons mirin

▲ **8 ounces firm tofu, drained and cut into ½-inch cubes**

▲ **½ English (seedless) cucumber, cut into matchstick strips**

4 (8 x 7-inch) sheets nori, cut into thin strips

1 avocado, halved, pitted, peeled, and sliced

2 tablespoons toasted sesame seeds

1 Cook rice according to package directions.

2 Stir together vinegar, soy sauce, and mirin in large bowl. Add hot cooked rice; toss to coat. Let stand, stirring occasionally, until cool.

3 Add tofu, cucumber, and nori to rice; toss to combine. Divide salad among 4 plates. Top evenly with avocado slices and sprinkle with sesame seeds.

Per serving (1 plate): 311 Cal, 11 g Total Fat, 2 g Sat Fat, 0 g Trans Fat, 0 mg Chol, 435 mg Sod, 44 g Carb, 2 g Sugar, 9 g Fib, 11 g Prot, 157 mg Calc.

FYI To toast sesame seeds, place them in a dry skillet and set over medium-low heat. Cook, stirring often, until the seeds are fragrant and lightly toasted, about 3 minutes. Transfer to a plate to cool.

bistro salad with egg

serves 4   ready in 20 minutes or less

½ cup plain low-fat yogurt

½ cup chopped fresh chives

1 tablespoon lime juice

1 clove garlic, minced

½ teaspoon salt

▲ 6 cups mixed baby salad greens

▲ 3 radishes, thinly sliced

▲ 2 large carrots, shredded

▲ 1 cup shredded red cabbage

2 teaspoons canola oil

▲ 4 large eggs

⅛ teaspoon black pepper

1 Combine yogurt, chives, lime juice, garlic, and salt in blender and puree.

2 Combine salad greens, radishes, carrots, and cabbage in large bowl. Add yogurt mixture and toss to coat. Divide salad among 4 plates.

3 Heat oil in large nonstick skillet over medium heat. Break eggs into skillet and cook until yolks just begin to set, 2–3 minutes. Sprinkle eggs with pepper. Top each salad with 1 egg. Serve at once.

Per serving (1 plate): 156 Cal, 8 g Total Fat, 2 g Sat Fat, 0 g Trans Fat, 188 mg Chol, 434 mg Sod, 11 g Carb, 6 g Sugar, 3 g Fib, 10 g Prot, 149 mg Calc.

CAN'T COMMIT? Top each salad with 1 ounce of diced skinless smoked chicken breast. The per-serving **PointsPlus** value will increase by **1**.

MOZZARELLA AND ARTICHOKE PITAS, PAGE 24, AND EDAMAME AND TOFU SLAW

edamame and tofu slaw

serves 4

△ **1 cup frozen shelled edamame**

¼ cup seasoned rice vinegar

1 tablespoon lime juice

1 tablespoon reduced-sodium soy sauce

2 teaspoons grated peeled fresh ginger

1 teaspoon honey

½ teaspoon Asian (dark) sesame oil

△ **4 ounces firm tofu, cut into ½-inch cubes**

△ **4 cups thinly sliced Napa cabbage**

△ **1 cup thinly sliced red cabbage**

△ **1 carrot, shredded**

△ **1 Kirby cucumber, peeled, halved, and thinly sliced**

1 Bring medium saucepan of water to boil over medium-high heat. Add edamame and cook 5 minutes. Drain, rinse under cold water, and pat dry.

2 Meanwhile, whisk together vinegar, lime juice, soy sauce, ginger, honey, and oil in large bowl. Add tofu and toss to coat. Set aside.

3 Add edamame, Napa cabbage, red cabbage, carrot, and cucumber to tofu mixture; toss to coat. Let stand at room temperature, tossing occasionally, 15 minutes.

Per serving (2 cups): 137 Cal, 4 g Total Fat, 1 g Sat Fat, 0 g Trans Fat, 0 mg Chol, 403 mg Sod, 18 g Carb, 11 g Sugar, 4 g Fib, 9 g Prot, 178 mg Calc.

chapter 3
stick-to-your-ribs dinners

grilled tofu kebabs with pineapple sauce

serves 4

4 teaspoons canola oil

▲ ½ fresh pineapple, peeled, cored, and sliced

¼ cup light (reduced-fat) coconut milk

2 teaspoons grated peeled fresh ginger

1 tablespoon honey

▲ 1 (14-ounce) package extra-firm tofu, drained and cut into 16 cubes

3 tablespoons reduced-sodium soy sauce

1 tablespoon chili-garlic paste

▲ 2 large zucchini, cut into 1-inch pieces

▲ 2 red bell peppers, cut into 1-inch pieces

▲ 1 red onion, cut into 1-inch pieces

1 Brush grill rack with 1 teaspoon oil. Preheat to medium-high or prepare medium-hot fire.

2 Brush pineapple with 1 teaspoon oil. Place on grill rack; grill, until lightly browned and tender, about 4 minutes on each side. Transfer to cutting board and let stand to cool. Coarsely chop pineapple.

3 To make sauce, puree pineapple, coconut milk, ginger, and honey in blender or food processor. Set aside.

4 Combine tofu, soy sauce, and chili-garlic paste in large bowl; toss to coat. Thread tofu, zucchini, bell peppers, and onion onto 8 (12-inch) metal skewers. Brush skewers with remaining 2 teaspoons oil.

5 Place skewers on grill rack; grill, turning occasionally, until vegetables are crisp-tender, about 8 minutes. Serve kebabs with sauce.

Per serving (2 kebabs and ¼ cup sauce): 280 Cal, 12 g Total Fat, 2 g Sat Fat, 0 g Trans Fat, 0 mg Chol, 516 mg Sod, 35 g Carb, 24 g Sugar, 6 g Fib, 14 g Prot, 230 mg Calc.

**GRILLED TOFU KEBABS
WITH PINEAPPLE SAUCE**

tofu "steaks" with onions and mushrooms

serves 4   ready in 20 minutes or less

- **4 teaspoons olive oil**
- ▲ **2 onions, thinly sliced**
- ▲ **½ pound white mushrooms, sliced**
- **3 teaspoons steak seasoning**
- **1 teaspoon fresh thyme leaves**
- ▲ **1 (14-ounce) package extra-firm tofu, drained**

1 Heat 2 teaspoons oil in large nonstick skillet over medium heat. Add onions and cook, stirring frequently, until lightly browned, about 5 minutes. Add mushrooms and 1 teaspoon steak seasoning. Cook, stirring frequently, until mushrooms are tender, about 5 minutes. Stir in thyme.

2 Meanwhile, coat nonstick grill pan with remaining 2 teaspoons oil; set over medium heat.

3 Cut tofu lengthwise in half; cut crosswise in half to make 4 "steaks." Sprinkle tofu with remaining 2 teaspoons steak seasoning. Add tofu to grill pan and grill until well marked and heated through, 3 minutes on each side. Serve with onions and mushrooms.

Per serving (1 tofu "steak" and ½ cup vegetables): 145 Cal, 11 g Total Fat, 1 g Sat Fat, 0 g Trans Fat, 0 mg Chol, 603 mg Sod, 9 g Carb, 4 g Sugar, 2 g Fib, 9 g Prot, 189 mg Calc.

STAY ON TRACK Serve this "steak" dinner with baked sweet potatoes. One medium baked sweet potato topped with 2 tablespoons plain fat-free Greek yogurt will increase the *PointsPlus* value by *3*.

hoisin-glazed tofu and vegetables with cashews

serves 4 ready in 20 minutes or less

1 cup reduced-sodium vegetable broth

2 tablespoons hoisin sauce

2 tablespoons reduced-sodium soy sauce

1 tablespoon rice vinegar

1 tablespoon cornstarch

1 tablespoon canola oil

2 tablespoons chopped peeled fresh ginger

2 garlic cloves, minced

1 (14-ounce) package firm tofu, drained and cut into bite-size pieces

1 (16-ounce) bag frozen Asian vegetable blend, thawed

2 tablespoons chopped unsalted cashews

1 Whisk together broth, hoisin sauce, soy sauce, vinegar, and cornstarch in small bowl.

2 Heat oil in large skillet or wok over medium-high heat. Add ginger and garlic and cook, stirring constantly, until fragrant, 1 minute. Stir broth mixture; add to skillet. Bring mixture to boil, stirring constantly. Add tofu and vegetables. Cook, stirring often, until heated through, 2 minutes. Sprinkle with cashews.

Per serving (1½ cups): 227 Cal, 12 g Total Fat, 1 g Sat Fat, 0 g Trans Fat, 0 mg Chol, 522 mg Sod, 20 g Carb, 5 g Sugar, 4 g Fib, 14 g Prot, 217 mg Calc.

STAY ON TRACK Soba noodles, made from buckwheat, are a flavorful and quick-cooking accompaniment to this dish. A ⅔-cup portion of cooked soba noodles per-serving will increase the **PointsPlus** value by **2**.

italian stuffed peppers with marinara sauce

serves 4

- ▲ **4 green or red bell peppers**
- ▲ **10 ounces reduced-fat firm tofu, cubed (about 2 cups)**
- ▲ **2 cups cooked brown rice**
- **½ cup shredded reduced-fat mozzarella cheese**
- **¼ cup golden raisins, chopped**
- **¼ cup thinly sliced fresh basil**
- ▲ **2 tablespoons chopped red onion**
- **2 tablespoons pine nuts**
- **2 cups prepared fat-free marinara sauce**

1 Preheat oven to 350°F. Cook bell peppers in large pot of boiling water until crisp-tender, about 2 minutes. Drain in colander; rinse under cold running water. Drain; cut off top of each bell pepper and remove seeds.

2 To make filling, combine tofu, rice, cheese, raisins, basil, onion, and pine nuts in large bowl. Toss to mix well.

3 Stuff filling evenly into each bell pepper. Place stuffed peppers in medium deep casserole or 1½-quart soufflé dish. Pour marinara sauce around peppers. Cover and bake, spooning marinara sauce over peppers once or twice, until peppers are tender and stuffing is heated through, about 45 minutes. Serve peppers with sauce.

Per serving (1 stuffed pepper with ¼ cup sauce): 326 Cal, 10 g Total Fat, 2 g Sat Fat, 0 g Trans Fat, 9 mg Chol, 606 mg Sod, 48 g Carb, 14 g Sugar, 9 g Fib, 15 g Prot, 210 mg Calc.

**ITALIAN STUFFED PEPPERS
WITH MARINARA SAUCE**

pad thai
with tofu and
vegetables

serves 4

6 ounces wide rice noodles

¼ cup tamarind juice

¼ cup reduced-sodium soy sauce

2 tablespoons demerara (raw) sugar

2 teaspoons canola oil

▲ ½ pound green beans, trimmed

▲ 2 carrots, shredded

▲ 1 small red onion, thinly sliced

2 garlic cloves, minced

2 teaspoons minced peeled fresh ginger

▲ 1 (14-ounce) package extra-firm tofu, drained

▲ 1 cup bean sprouts

▲ 1 scallion, thinly sliced

Chopped fresh cilantro or basil

1 Cook rice noodles according to package directions, omitting salt if desired. Drain.

2 Combine tamarind juice, soy sauce, and sugar in small saucepan; set over medium heat. Cook, stirring constantly, until sugar dissolves. Set aside.

3 Heat oil in wok or large skillet over medium-high heat until a drop of water sizzles on pan. Add green beans, carrots, onion, and garlic. Stir-fry until vegetables are crisp-tender, 3–4 minutes. Add tofu, rice noodles, bean sprouts, and tamarind juice mixture to wok. Stir-fry until noodles and tofu are heated through, 1–2 minutes. Sprinkle with scallion and cilantro.

Per serving (1¾ cups): 374 Cal, 10 g Total Fat, 1 g Sat Fat, 0 g Trans Fat, 0 mg Chol, 776 mg Sod, 60 g Carb, 14 g Sugar, 5 g Fib, 16 g Prot, 237 mg Calc.

CAN'T COMMIT? To add beef to this dish, trim ½ pound lean sirloin steak and cut it into ¼-inch-thick strips. Heat the oil as directed in step 3. Add the steak and stir-fry 2–3 minutes. Transfer to plate. Proceed with the recipe, returning the steak to the wok during the last minute of cooking. The per-serving **PointsPlus** value will increase by **2**.

gingery tempeh and green bean stir-fry

serves 4   ready in 20 minutes or less

¾ cup water

3 tablespoons hoisin sauce

2 tablespoons mirin

2 tablespoons reduced-sodium soy sauce

2 teaspoons cornstarch

▲ 1½ pounds green beans, trimmed

1 tablespoon canola oil

3 tablespoons chopped peeled fresh ginger

4 garlic cloves, minced

8 ounces tempeh, cut into cubes

1 teaspoon Asian (dark) sesame oil

1 tablespoon sesame seeds, toasted

1 Whisk together water, hoisin sauce, mirin, soy sauce, and cornstarch in small bowl.

2 Bring large saucepan of water to boil. Add green beans. Return to boil and cook until green beans are just crisp-tender, 2 minutes. Drain.

3 Meanwhile, heat canola oil in large skillet over medium-high heat. Add ginger and garlic; cook, stirring constantly, until fragrant, 1 minute. Stir hoisin sauce mixture and add to skillet. Add tempeh. Stir-fry until sauce bubbles and thickens, 3 minutes.

4 Add green beans; stir-fry until heated through, 1 minute. Stir in sesame oil and sprinkle with sesame seeds.

Per serving (1¾ cups): 271 Cal, 13 g Total Fat, 2 g Sat Fat, 0 g Trans Fat, 0 mg Chol, 480 mg Sod, 28 g Carb, 8 g Sugar, 7 g Fib, 15 g Prot, 135 mg Calc.

STAY ON TRACK   Brown rice is a healthful and filling side for this stir-fry; ½ cup of cooked brown rice per serving will increase the *PointsPlus* value by *3*.

TEMPEH AND MUSHROOM BOLOGNESE

tempeh and mushroom bolognese

serves 4 ready in 20 minutes or less

- ½ pound whole wheat fettuccine
- 3 teaspoons olive oil
- ½ pound tempeh
- ¼ cup water
- 1 onion, chopped
- ½ pound white mushrooms, sliced
- 4 garlic cloves, minced
- 1 (28-ounce) can crushed tomatoes
- ½ cup fat-free half-and-half
- ¼ cup packed fresh basil leaves, torn if large
- 4 teaspoons grated Parmesan

1 Cook fettuccine according to package directions, omitting salt if desired.

2 Meanwhile, heat 1 teaspoon oil in medium nonstick skillet over medium heat. Add tempeh and cook until lightly browned, about 2 minutes on each side. Add water and cook, using a wooden spoon to break up tempeh, about 3 minutes longer. Transfer to plate.

3 Add remaining 2 teaspoons oil to skillet. Add onion, mushrooms, and garlic. Cook, stirring occasionally, until vegetables are softened, 5 minutes. Add tomatoes and tempeh; bring to boil. Cook, stirring occasionally, until sauce is slightly thickened, 5 minutes. Stir in half-and-half and basil. Divide fettuccine among 4 plates. Top evenly with sauce and sprinkle with cheese.

Per serving (1 cup pasta, 1½ cups sauce, and 1 teaspoon cheese): 453 Cal, 11 g Total Fat, 2 g Sat Fat, 0 g Trans Fat, 1 mg Chol, 554 mg Sod, 68 g Carb, 12 g Sugar, 11 g Fib, 25 g Prot, 229 mg Calc.

black bean, barley, and sweet potato chili

serves 4

- ▲ **¾ cup pearl barley**
- **1 tablespoon olive oil**
- ▲ **1 large onion, chopped**
- **4 garlic cloves, minced**
- **1½ teaspoons ancho chile powder**
- **1 teaspoon dried oregano**
- **½ teaspoon ground cumin**
- ▲ **3 sweet potatoes, peeled and cut into ½-inch cubes**
- ▲ **2 green bell peppers, diced**
- ▲ **1 (14½-ounce) can diced tomatoes**
- **2 cups water**
- **½ teaspoon salt**
- ▲ **1 (15-ounce) can black beans, rinsed and drained**
- **Chopped fresh cilantro**
- **Lime wedges**

1 Cook barley according to package directions.

2 Meanwhile, heat oil in large saucepan over medium-high heat. Add onion and cook, stirring occasionally, until softened, about 5 minutes. Add garlic, chile powder, oregano, and cumin. Cook, stirring constantly, until fragrant, 1 minute.

3 Add sweet potatoes, bell peppers, tomatoes, water, and salt; bring to boil. Reduce heat and cover. Simmer until sweet potatoes are tender, about 20 minutes. Stir in barley and beans. Cook until heated through, 3 minutes.

4 Divide chili among 4 bowls. Sprinkle with cilantro and serve with lime wedges.

Per serving (2¾ cups): 406 Cal, 5 g Total Fat, 1 g Sat Fat, 0 g Trans Fat, 0 mg Chol, 773 mg Sod, 81 g Carb, 13 g Sugar, 20 g Fib, 14 g Prot, 157 mg Calc.

FYI Ancho chile powder is made from dried ground poblano chiles. It gives this chili gentle heat and complex flavor, but the dish will still be delicious if you make it with regular chili powder.

curried edamame and vegetables

serves 4 ready in 20 minutes or less

△ **1 pound green beans, trimmed**

1 tablespoon canola oil

3 garlic cloves, minced

2 tablespoons Thai green curry paste

△ **2 cups reduced-sodium vegetable broth**

1 cup light (reduced-fat) coconut milk

2 teaspoons reduced-sodium soy sauce

1 teaspoon sugar

△ **2 red bell peppers, thinly sliced**

△ **1 large carrot, cut into matchstick strips**

△ **1½ cups frozen shelled edamame, thawed**

△ **2 cups hot cooked brown rice**

¼ cup thinly sliced fresh basil

Lime wedges

1 Bring large saucepan of water to boil. Add green beans. Return to boil and cook until green beans are just crisp-tender, 2 minutes. Drain.

2 Meanwhile, heat oil in large skillet over medium-high heat. Add garlic and curry paste; cook, stirring constantly, until fragrant, 1 minute. Add broth, coconut milk, soy sauce, and sugar; bring to boil. Reduce heat and simmer 2 minutes. Add bell peppers and carrot. Cook, stirring occasionally, until vegetables are crisp-tender, 3 minutes. Add green beans and edamame; cook, stirring often, until heated through, 2 minutes.

3 Divide rice among 4 bowls; top evenly with curry. Sprinkle with sliced basil and serve with lime wedges.

Per serving (2 cups curry and ½ cup rice): 320 Cal, 11 g Total Fat, 3 g Sat Fat, 0 g Trans Fat, 0 mg Chol, 745 mg Sod, 48 g Carb, 13 g Sugar, 11 g Fib, 13 g Prot, 111 mg Calc.

tvp stuffed mushrooms

serves 4

- 5 large portobello mushrooms, stems removed
- 2 teaspoons olive oil
- 3 ounces shiitake mushrooms, stems removed and caps sliced
- 1 carrot, diced
- 1 small onion, chopped
- 2 garlic cloves, minced
- 1¼ cups reduced-sodium vegetable broth
- ¾ cup textured vegetable protein (TVP)
- ¼ teaspoon black pepper
- ¼ cup grated Parmesan cheese
- 2 tablespoons lemon juice
- 2 tablespoons chopped fresh basil
- 1 cup prepared fat-free marinara sauce
- 1 cup shredded reduced-fat mozzarella cheese

1 Preheat broiler. Spray large baking sheet with cooking spray. Using small spoon, scrape out and discard dark gills from underside of 4 mushrooms. Place mushrooms on baking sheet and broil until tender, about 3 minutes on each side.

2 Preheat oven to 400°F.

3 Meanwhile, chop remaining portobello mushroom cap. Heat oil in large nonstick skillet over medium heat. Add chopped portobello mushroom, shiitake mushrooms, carrot, onion, and garlic and cook, stirring occasionally, until vegetables are tender, about 8 minutes.

4 Add vegetable broth, vegetable protein, and pepper; bring to boil. Reduce heat and cover. Simmer until broth is absorbed, about 5 minutes. Remove from heat and stir in Parmesan, lemon juice, and basil.

5 Mound mushroom mixture into mushroom caps. Top with marinara sauce and mozzarella. Bake until filling is heated through and cheese melts, 10–15 minutes.

Per serving (1 stuffed mushroom): 272 Cal, 11 g Total Fat, 5 g Sat Fat, 0 g Trans Fat, 20 mg Chol, 708 mg Sod, 17 g Carb, 9 g Sugar, 4 g Fib, 29 g Prot, 358 mg Calc.

penne with chunky tvp-marinara sauce

serves 4

- ▲ ½ **pound whole wheat penne**
- **2 teaspoons olive oil**
- ▲ **1 green bell pepper, chopped**
- ▲ **1 onion, chopped**
- ½ **cup textured vegetable protein (TVP)**
- **2 garlic cloves, minced**
- ▲ **1 (14½-ounce) can diced tomatoes**
- ▲ **1 (8-ounce) can tomato sauce**
- ½ **cup water**
- ½ **teaspoon dried oregano**
- ¼ **teaspoon black pepper**
- **Pinch crushed red pepper flakes**
- **2 tablespoons chopped fresh basil**
- ¼ **cup grated Parmesan**

1 Cook penne according to package directions, omitting salt if desired.

2 Meanwhile, heat oil in medium skillet over medium-high heat. Add bell pepper and onion and cook, stirring occasionally, until softened, 5 minutes. Add vegetable protein and garlic and cook, stirring constantly, until vegetable protein is lightly browned, 3 minutes.

3 Add tomatoes, tomato sauce, water, oregano, pepper, and pepper flakes and bring to boil. Reduce heat and cover. Simmer until sauce is slightly thickened, 15 minutes. Stir in basil.

4 Divide pasta among 4 plates; top evenly with sauce. Sprinkle with Parmesan.

Per serving (1½ cups pasta, generous ½ cup sauce, and 1 tablespoon cheese): 339 Cal, 6 g Total Fat, 2 g Sat Fat, 0 g Trans Fat, 5 mg Chol, 782 mg Sod, 54 g Carb, 8 g Sugar, 8 g Fib, 24 g Prot, 181 mg Calc.

"NACHO" FRITTATA

"nacho" frittata

serves 4 ready in 20 minutes or less

▲ **4 large eggs**

▲ **1 cup frozen corn kernels, thawed**

▲ **1 cup reduced-sodium fat-free salsa**

6 tablespoons light sour cream

½ cup shredded reduced-fat Mexican cheese blend

▲ **2 scallions, thinly sliced**

▲ **2 tablespoons cornmeal**

1 tablespoon canola oil

▲ **1 cup fat-free refried beans, heated**

▲ **2 plum tomatoes, chopped**

¼ cup chopped fresh cilantro

1 Preheat oven to 400°F.

2 Whisk together eggs, corn, ½ cup salsa, 3 tablespoons sour cream, ¼ cup Mexican cheese blend, scallions, and cornmeal in large bowl.

3 Heat oil in large ovenproof nonstick skillet over medium heat. Add egg mixture and cook until edge begins to set, 2 minutes. Place frittata in oven and bake until center is set, 8–10 minutes.

4 Transfer frittata to large plate. Top with dollops of beans, remaining ½ cup salsa, and remaining 3 tablespoons sour cream. Sprinkle with tomatoes, cilantro, and remaining ¼ cup cheese.

Per serving (¼ of frittata with "nacho" toppings): 301 Cal, 15 g Total Fat, 5 g Sat Fat, 0 g Trans Fat, 203 mg Chol, 481 mg Sod, 27 g Carb, 6 g Sugar, 5 g Fib, 16 g Prot, 195 mg Calc.

italian potato torta with spinach and cheese

serves 4

▲ **1½ pounds small Yukon Gold potatoes**

2 tablespoons Italian-seasoned dried bread crumbs

2 teaspoons olive oil

4 garlic cloves, minced

▲ **1 (6-ounce) package baby spinach**

▲ **2 large eggs**

▲ **½ cup fat-free milk**

¼ teaspoon salt

¼ teaspoon ground nutmeg

⅛ teaspoon black pepper

1 cup shredded reduced-fat Italian cheese blend

1 Place potatoes in medium saucepan and cover with water. Bring to boil and simmer until tender, about 20 minutes. Drain; transfer to large bowl and mash.

2 Preheat oven to 375°F. Spray 9-inch glass pie plate with nonstick spray; sprinkle with bread crumbs.

3 Heat oil in large nonstick skillet over medium heat. Add garlic; cook, stirring constantly until fragrant, 1 minute. Add spinach; cook, stirring constantly, until wilted, 2 minutes. Add spinach mixture to potatoes and stir to combine. Let cool slightly.

4 Whisk together eggs, milk, salt, nutmeg, and pepper in medium bowl. Stir in ¾ cup Italian cheese blend. Add egg mixture to potato mixture and stir to combine. Spoon potato mixture into prepared pie plate.

5 Bake until torta is heated through and lightly browned, about 25 minutes. Sprinkle torta with remaining ¼ cup cheese. Bake until cheese melts, about 3 minutes longer.

Per serving (¼ of torta): 299 Cal, 10 g Total Fat, 4 g Sat Fat, 0 g Trans Fat, 112 mg Chol, 457 mg Sod, 38 g Carb, 4 g Sugar, 5 g Fib, 15 g Prot, 324 mg Calc.

brie and tomato bread pudding

serves 6

2 teaspoons olive oil

▲ 1 onion, chopped

▲ 1 red bell pepper, chopped

▲ 1½ cups grape tomatoes, halved

½ pound whole wheat French bread, cut into cubes

¼ pound Brie, cut into small cubes

▲ 6 large eggs

▲ 2 cups fat-free milk

1 tablespoon Dijon mustard

2 teaspoons fresh thyme leaves

¼ teaspoon salt

¼ teaspoon black pepper

1 Preheat oven to 350°F. Spray 9 x 13-inch baking dish with nonstick spray.

2 Heat oil in large skillet over medium-high heat. Add onion and bell pepper. Cook, stirring occasionally, until softened, 5 minutes. Remove from heat. Stir in tomatoes and bread cubes. Transfer mixture to prepared baking dish; sprinkle evenly with Brie.

3 Whisk together eggs, milk, mustard, thyme, salt, and black pepper in medium bowl. Add egg mixture to baking dish; press bread cubes to submerge into egg mixture. Let stand 10 minutes.

4 Bake 15 minutes. Remove from oven and press bread cubes into egg mixture with spatula. Return to oven and bake until bread pudding is puffed and golden, about 20 minutes longer. Let stand 10 minutes before serving.

Per serving (⅙ of casserole): 300 Cal, 14 g Total Fat, 6 g Sat Fat, 0 g Trans Fat, 207 mg Chol, 558 mg Sod, 25 g Carb, 11 g Sugar, 4 g Fib, 19 g Prot, 213 mg Calc.

FYI This bread pudding can be prepared the day before serving through step 3. Cover and refrigerate. Uncover and let stand at room temperature 15 minutes before baking. You may need to add an additional 10 minutes to the baking time.

chickpea pot pie

serves 6

2 teaspoons olive oil

▲ ½ pound small white mushrooms, quartered

▲ 2 carrots, chopped

▲ 2 celery stalks, chopped

▲ 1 onion, chopped

▲ 1 green bell pepper, chopped

2 garlic cloves, minced

▲ 3 cups reduced-sodium vegetable broth

3 tablespoons cornstarch

2 ounces reduced-fat cream cheese, softened

▲ 1 (15-ounce) can chickpeas, rinsed and drained

2 tablespoons chopped fresh sage

½ teaspoon salt

1 refrigerated pie crust (from 14.1-ounce package)

1 Preheat oven to 400°F. Spray 9-inch pie plate with nonstick spray.

2 Heat oil in large skillet over medium-high heat. Add mushrooms, carrots, celery, onion, bell pepper, and garlic. Cook, stirring occasionally, until vegetables are softened, about 8 minutes. Stir together broth and cornstarch in medium bowl until blended. Add to skillet. Cook, stirring constantly, until mixture comes to boil and thickens, 2 minutes. Add cream cheese; cook, stirring until smooth, 1 minute. Stir in chickpeas, sage, and salt. Spoon chickpea mixture into prepared pie plate.

3 Place pie crust over filling; press edges with fork to form decorative edge. With knife, make several 1-inch slits in top of crust. Place pie on baking sheet. Bake until crust is golden and filling is bubbling, 25–30 minutes. Let stand about 10 minutes before serving.

Per serving (⅙ of pie): 311 Cal, 14 g Total Fat, 5 g Sat Fat, 0 g Trans Fat, 9 mg Chol, 736 mg Sod, 42 g Carb, 5 g Sugar, 5 g Fib, 8 g Prot, 64 mg Calc.

CHICKPEA POT PIE

chickpea and farro stew with rosemary

serves 4

2 teaspoons olive oil

▲ 1 cup farro

▲ 1 large onion, chopped

2 teaspoons minced fresh rosemary

2 teaspoons ground cumin

2 teaspoons paprika

▲ 5 cups reduced-sodium vegetable broth

▲ 1 (28-ounce) can no-salt-added crushed tomatoes

▲ 2 (15-ounce) cans chickpeas, rinsed and drained

¼ teaspoon black pepper

Grated zest of 1 lemon

Chopped fresh flat-leaf parsley

1 Heat oil in large saucepan over medium-high heat. Add farro, onion, rosemary, cumin, and paprika; cook, stirring constantly, until fragrant, 1 minute.

2 Add broth, tomatoes, and chickpeas; bring to boil. Reduce heat and cover. Simmer until farro is tender, 30–45 minutes. Stir in pepper.

3 Ladle stew into 4 bowls; top with lemon zest and parsley.

Per serving (about 1¼ cups): 524 Cal, 8 g Total Fat, 1 g Sat Fat, 0 g Trans Fat, 0 mg Chol, 765 mg Sod, 95 g Carb, 14 g Sugar, 18 g Fib, 22 g Prot, 181 mg Calc.

CAN'T COMMIT? To add lamb to this stew, trim ½ pound lean boneless lamb shoulder and cut it into ½-inch cubes. Heat the oil as directed in step 1. Add the lamb and cook, stirring often, until browned, about 6 minutes. Proceed with the recipe, substituting beef broth for the vegetable broth. The per-serving *PointsPlus* value will increase by **4**.

vegetable korma

serves 4

1 tablespoon canola oil

1 onion, sliced

2 tablespoons chopped peeled fresh ginger

4 garlic cloves, minced

2 teaspoons garam masala

¼ teaspoon salt

1 (8-ounce) can tomato sauce

1 cup water

1 small head broccoli, cut into florets

1 small head cauliflower, cut into florets

2 carrots, thinly sliced

1 (15-ounce) can chickpeas, rinsed and drained

¼ cup raisins

¼ cup fat-free half-and-half

2 cups cooked brown basmati rice

2 tablespoons slivered almonds, toasted

1 Heat oil in large saucepan over medium-high heat. Add onion and cook, stirring occasionally, until softened, 5 minutes. Add ginger, garlic, garam masala, and salt. Cook, stirring constantly, until fragrant, 1 minute.

2 Add tomato sauce, water, broccoli, cauliflower, and carrots; bring to boil. Reduce heat and simmer until vegetables are tender, 10–15 minutes, adding chickpeas and raisins during last 5 minutes of cooking time. Remove from heat; stir in half-and-half.

3 Divide rice among 4 bowls. Top evenly with korma and sprinkle with almonds.

Per serving (2 cups korma, ½ cup rice, and ½ tablespoon almonds): 432 Cal, 10 g Total Fat, 1 g Sat Fat, 0 g Trans Fat, 1 mg Chol, 659 mg Sod, 76 g Carb, 16 g Sugar, 16 g Fib, 17 g Prot, 190 mg Calc.

CAN'T COMMIT? Add 2 cups shredded skinless cooked chicken breast when you add the chickpeas in step 2. The per-serving *PointsPlus* value will increase by *3*.

white bean and roasted ratatouille stew

serves 4

- ▲ **2 zucchini, quartered lengthwise and thickly sliced**
- ▲ **2 small eggplants (about 1 pound), quartered lengthwise and thickly sliced**
- ▲ **1 red bell pepper, cut into ½-inch pieces**
- ▲ **1 red onion, cut into thin wedges**
- **4 teaspoons olive oil**
- **4 garlic cloves, minced**
- ▲ **2 (14½-ounce) cans diced tomatoes**
- ▲ **1 (15-ounce) can cannellini (white kidney) beans, undrained**
- **⅛ teaspoon black pepper**
- **⅛ teaspoon red pepper flakes**
- **¼ cup chopped fresh basil**
- ▲ **½ pound whole wheat pasta shells**
- **2 tablespoons grated Parmesan**

1 Preheat oven to 400°F. Spray large rimmed baking sheet with nonstick spray. Place zucchini, eggplants, bell pepper, and onion on prepared baking sheet. Drizzle with 2 teaspoons oil and toss to coat. Arrange vegetables in single layer. Roast, stirring once, until vegetables are lightly browned and tender, 30–35 minutes.

2 Heat remaining 2 teaspoons oil in large skillet over medium-high heat. Add garlic and cook, stirring constantly, until fragrant, 1 minute. Add tomatoes and cook, stirring occasionally, until liquid is slightly reduced, 5 minutes. Add roasted vegetables, beans, black pepper, and pepper flakes. Cook, stirring occasionally, until heated through, about 5 minutes. Remove from heat and stir in basil.

3 Meanwhile, cook pasta according to package directions, omitting salt if desired.

4 Divide pasta among 4 bowls. Top evenly with stew and sprinkle with cheese.

Per serving (1½ cups stew, 1 cup pasta, and ½ tablespoon cheese): 452 Cal, 7 g Total Fat, 2 g Sat Fat, 0 g Trans Fat, 2 mg Chol, 797 mg Sod, 83 g Carb, 14 g Sugar, 17 g Fib, 21 g Prot, 239 mg Calc.

curried rice, beans, and butternut squash

serves 4

 1 butternut squash (2 pounds), peeled, seeded, and cut into 1-inch pieces

4 teaspoons canola oil

½ teaspoon salt

⅛ teaspoon black pepper

 1 onion, chopped

2 tablespoons chopped peeled fresh ginger

3 garlic cloves, minced

2 cups water

 1 cup brown rice

2 teaspoons hot curry powder

½ teaspoon ground allspice

 1 (15-ounce) can black beans, rinsed and drained

 ½ bunch kale, trimmed and thinly sliced

 1 jalapeño pepper, seeded and minced

1 Preheat oven to 425°F. Spray large rimmed baking sheet with nonstick spray.

2 Place squash on prepared baking sheet. Drizzle with 2 teaspoons oil and sprinkle with ¼ teaspoon salt and black pepper; toss to coat. Arrange squash in single layer. Roast, stirring once, until squash is lightly browned and tender, 35–40 minutes.

3 Meanwhile, heat remaining 2 teaspoons oil in large saucepan over medium-high heat. Add onion, ginger, and garlic. Cook, stirring occasionally, until onion begins to soften, 3 minutes. Stir in water, rice, curry powder, allspice, and remaining ¼ teaspoon salt; bring to boil. Reduce heat and cover. Simmer, stirring occasionally, until rice is tender, about 30 minutes.

4 Stir in beans, kale, and jalapeño. Cook, stirring occasionally, until heated through, 5 minutes. Gently stir in roasted squash.

Per serving (2 cups): 425 Cal, 7 g Total Fat, 1 g Sat Fat, 0 g Trans Fat, 0 mg Chol, 596 mg Sod, 82 g Carb, 9 g Sugar, 19 g Fib, 13 g Prot, 203 mg Calc.

BEAN, MUSHROOM, AND CORN
ENCHILADAS

bean, mushroom, and corn enchiladas

serves 4

2 teaspoons canola oil

▲ ½ pound cremini mushrooms, sliced

▲ 1 onion, chopped

▲ 1 poblano pepper, thinly sliced

▲ 1 (10-ounce) package frozen corn kernels, thawed

▲ 1 (15-ounce) can pinto beans, rinsed, drained, and lightly mashed

▲ 1¼ cups fat-free salsa verde

1 teaspoon ground cumin

8 (6-inch) corn tortillas, warmed

¼ cup water

1 cup shredded reduced-fat Mexican cheese blend

1 Preheat oven to 400°F. Spray 9 x 13-inch baking dish with nonstick spray.

2 Heat oil in large skillet over medium-high heat. Add mushrooms, onion, and poblano. Cook, stirring occasionally, until vegetables are tender, 8 minutes. Add corn, beans, ¾ cup salsa verde, and cumin. Cook, stirring often, until heated through, 3 minutes.

3 Lay tortillas on work surface and spoon about ½ cup mushroom mixture on top. Roll up each tortilla to enclose filling. Place enchiladas, seam side down, in prepared baking dish.

4 Sprinkle water over enchiladas; top with remaining ½ cup salsa verde. Sprinkle with Mexican cheese blend. Cover and bake until enchiladas are heated through and cheese is melted, about 15 minutes.

11 PointsPlus® value

Per serving (2 enchiladas): 422 Cal, 11 g Total Fat, 4 g Sat Fat, 0 g Trans Fat, 15 mg Chol, 571 mg Sod, 66 g Carb, 8 g Sugar, 13 g Fib, 21 g Prot, 314 mg Calc.

FYI Lightly mashing the beans softens their texture and helps keep them inside the tortillas. To mash them, place the beans in a bowl and mash with a potato masher or a fork.

winter vegetable and lentil tagine

serves 4

- **1 tablespoon canola oil**
- **1 onion, sliced**
- **½ teaspoon hot curry powder**
- **½ teaspoon ground cumin**
- **½ teaspoon paprika**
- **¼ teaspoon cinnamon**
- **¼ teaspoon black pepper**
- **3 cups reduced-sodium vegetable broth**
- **1 (8-ounce) can tomato sauce**
- **2 sweet potatoes, peeled and cut into ½-inch cubes**
- **2 turnips, peeled, quartered, and sliced**
- **1 large carrot, quartered lengthwise and sliced**
- **1 parsnip, peeled, quartered lengthwise, and sliced**
- **½ cup red lentils, picked over and rinsed**
- **½ cup mixed dried fruit, diced**
- **2 tablespoons lemon juice**
- **2 tablespoons chopped fresh parsley**

1 Heat oil in large saucepan over medium-high heat. Add onion and cook, stirring occasionally, until softened, 5 minutes.

2 Add curry powder, cumin, paprika, cinnamon, and pepper. Cook, stirring constantly, until fragrant, 1 minute. Stir in broth, tomato sauce, sweet potatoes, turnips, carrot, parsnip, lentils, and dried fruit; bring to boil. Reduce heat and cover. Simmer until vegetables are tender, about 20 minutes. Remove from heat. Stir in lemon juice and parsley.

Per serving (2 cups): 286 Cal, 4 g Total Fat, 0 g Sat Fat, 0 g Trans Fat, 0 mg Chol, 714 mg Sod, 56 g Carb, 23 g Sugar, 12 g Fib, 10 g Prot, 100 mg Calc.

STAY ON TRACK   Whole wheat couscous is a natural complement to this Middle Eastern dish. A ½ cup cooked couscous per serving will increase the *PointsPlus* value by *3*.

lentil and mushroom nut loaf

serves 6

loaf

3 cups water

▲ 1¼ cups brown lentils, picked over and rinsed

▲ 1 onion, chopped

▲ ¼ pound white mushrooms, chopped

▲ ½ green bell pepper, chopped

½ cup unsalted mixed nuts, chopped

3 tablespoons plain dried bread crumbs

▲ 3 large egg whites

4 garlic cloves, minced

½ teaspoon salt

¼ teaspoon black pepper

sauce

1 teaspoon olive oil

▲ ½ onion, chopped

2 garlic cloves, minced

▲ 1 (14½-ounce) can diced tomatoes

¼ teaspoon salt

⅛ teaspoon black pepper

¼ cup chopped fresh flat-leaf parsley

1 To make loaf, bring water and lentils to boil in large saucepan. Reduce heat and simmer, partially covered, until lentils are tender, about 20 minutes. Drain. Transfer lentils to large bowl.

2 Preheat oven to 350°F. Spray 4 x 8-inch loaf pan with nonstick spray.

3 Add onion, mushrooms, bell pepper, nuts, bread crumbs, egg whites, garlic, salt, and black pepper to lentils; stir to combine. Spoon lentil mixture into prepared pan. Bake until loaf is lightly browned, 40 minutes. Remove from oven and let stand 15 minutes. Cut into 6 slices in pan.

4 Meanwhile to make sauce, heat oil in small saucepan over medium heat. Add onion and garlic; cook, stirring occasionally, until onion is softened, 5 minutes. Add tomatoes, salt, and pepper; simmer 5 minutes. Remove from heat and stir in parsley. Serve loaf with sauce.

Per serving (⅙ of loaf and ⅓ cup sauce): 259 Cal, 7 g Total Fat, 1 g Sat Fat, 0 g Trans Fat, 0 mg Chol, 458 mg Sod, 35 g Carb, 5 g Sugar, 9 g Fib, 16 g Prot, 79 mg Calc.

veggie jambalaya

serves 4

2 teaspoons olive oil

▲ 4 celery stalks, thinly sliced

▲ 2 carrots, thinly sliced

▲ 2 onions, chopped

▲ 1 red bell pepper, diced

4 garlic cloves, minced

¾ teaspoon dried thyme

⅛ teaspoon cayenne

2 cups water

¾ cup long-grain white rice

▲ ¾ cup red lentils, picked over and rinsed

▲ 1 (14½-ounce) can stewed tomatoes

¾ teaspoon salt

▲ 1 (10-ounce) package frozen corn kernels, thawed

¼ cup chopped fresh parsley

1 Heat oil in large saucepan over medium-high heat. Add celery, carrots, onions, and bell pepper. Cook, stirring occasionally, until vegetables are softened, 8 minutes. Add garlic, thyme, and cayenne; cook, stirring constantly, 1 minute.

2 Stir in water, rice, lentils, tomatoes, and salt; bring to boil. Reduce heat and cover. Simmer, stirring occasionally, until rice and lentils are tender, about 20 minutes.

3 Add corn and cook 5 minutes longer. Stir in parsley.

Per serving (2 cups): 386 Cal, 4 g Total Fat, 1 g Sat Fat, 0 g Trans Fat, 0 mg Chol, 657 mg Sod, 78 g Carb, 11 g Sugar, 12 g Fib, 15 g Prot, 118 mg Calc.

CAN'T COMMIT? Stir in ½ pound peeled and deveined medium shrimp when you add the corn in step 3. The per-serving *PointsPlus* value will increase by *1*.

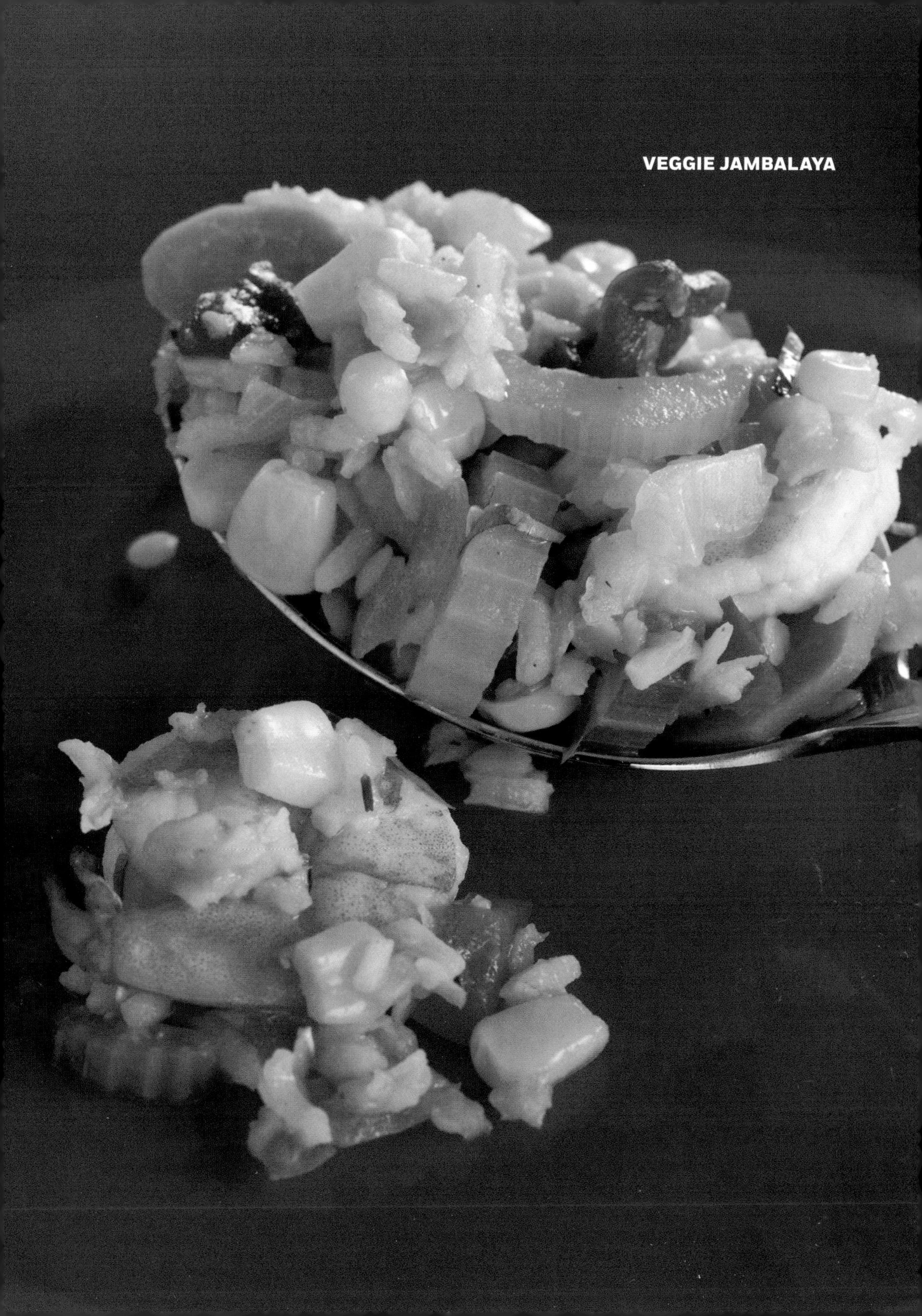

VEGGIE JAMBALAYA

chipotle lentil chili with brown rice

serves 8

2 teaspoons olive oil
△ 1 onion, chopped
△ 1 green bell pepper, chopped
△ 2 carrots, chopped
4 garlic cloves, minced
3 tablespoons chili powder
1 tablespoon ground cumin
2 teaspoons dried oregano
1 teaspoon chipotle chile powder
7 cups water
△ 2 cups brown lentils, picked over and rinsed
△ 1 (14½-ounce) can diced fire-roasted tomatoes
¾ teaspoon salt
△ 1½ cups brown rice
Chopped fresh cilantro
△ Thinly sliced scallions
Lime wedges

1 Heat oil in large saucepan over medium-high heat. Add onion, bell pepper, carrots, and garlic. Cook, stirring occasionally, until vegetables are softened, 6 minutes. Add chili powder, cumin, oregano, and chipotle chile powder; cook, stirring constantly, 1 minute.

2 Add water, lentils, tomatoes, and salt; bring to boil. Reduce heat and simmer, partially covered, stirring occasionally, until lentils are tender, about 20 minutes.

3 Meanwhile, cook rice according to package directions.

4 Spoon rice into 8 serving bowls; evenly ladle chili over rice. Sprinkle with cilantro and scallions, and serve with lime wedges.

Per serving (1¼ cups chili and ½ cup brown rice): 333 Cal, 3 g Total Fat, 1 g Sat Fat, 0 g Trans Fat, 0 mg Chol, 424 mg Sod, 62 g Carb, 4 g Sugar, 14 g Fib, 16 g Prot, 94 mg Calc.

pasta with white beans, onions, and escarole

serves 4

1 tablespoon olive oil

▲ 2 onions, thinly sliced

▲ 1 bunch escarole, cleaned and coarsely chopped

⅓ cup golden raisins

▲ 1 (15-ounce) can cannellini (white kidney) beans, undrained

¼ teaspoon salt

¼ teaspoon red pepper flakes

▲ ½ pound whole wheat rotini

2 tablespoons grated Romano or Parmesan

1 Heat oil in large nonstick skillet over medium heat. Add onions. Cover and cook, stirring occasionally, until onions are golden, about 15 minutes.

2 Add escarole and raisins. Cover and cook, stirring occasionally, until escarole is tender, about 5 minutes. Stir in beans and their liquid, salt, and pepper flakes; bring to boil. Cook, uncovered, until heated through, 2 minutes.

3 Meanwhile, cook pasta according to package directions, omitting salt if desired. Drain, reserving 1 cup cooking water.

4 Add pasta to onion mixture, adding pasta cooking water, ¼ cup at time, until mixture is moistened. Divide among 4 shallow bowls; sprinkle evenly with cheese.

Per serving (2 cups pasta mixture and ½ tablespoon cheese): 402 Cal, 6 g Total Fat, 1 g Sat Fat, 0 g Trans Fat, 4 mg Chol, 707 mg Sod, 76 g Carb, 11 g Sugar, 11 g Fib, 18 g Prot, 162 mg Calc.

penne with chickpeas and sundried tomatoes

serves 4

- ½ pound whole wheat penne
- 1 tablespoon olive oil
- 10 oil-packed sundried tomatoes, drained and patted dry with paper towels, and thinly sliced
- 4 garlic cloves, thinly sliced
- ¼ teaspoon red pepper flakes
- 1 (15-ounce) can chickpeas, rinsed and drained
- 1 (6-ounce) package baby spinach
- ¼ teaspoon salt
- 2 tablespoons grated Parmesan

1 Cook penne according to package directions, omitting salt if desired. Drain, reserving 1 cup cooking water.

2 Meanwhile, heat oil in large nonstick skillet over medium heat. Add tomatoes, garlic, and pepper flakes; cook, stirring constantly, 1 minute.

3 Stir in chickpeas, pasta cooking water, spinach, and salt. Cook until beans are heated through and spinach wilts, about 2 minutes. Stir in penne.

4 Divide among 4 shallow bowls; sprinkle evenly with Parmesan.

Per serving (2 cups pasta mixture and ½ tablespoon cheese): 405 Cal, 9 g Total Fat, 2 g Sat Fat, 0 g Trans Fat, 2 mg Chol, 632 mg Sod, 68 g Carb, 5 g Sugar, 11 g Fib, 18 g Prot, 157 mg Calc.

CAN'T COMMIT? Cook 8 ounces Italian turkey sausages in 2 teaspoons olive oil in a skillet over medium heat, until no longer pink in center, 8 minutes. Thinly slice the sausages. Add to the skillet with the penne in step 3. The per-serving *PointsPlus* value will increase by *2*.

gemelli and limas with arugula pesto

serves 4

¼ cup fresh whole wheat bread crumbs

△ ½ pound whole wheat gemelli or penne

△ 1 (10-ounce) package frozen baby lima beans, thawed

△ 1½ cups loosely packed baby arugula

1 cup loosely packed fresh basil leaves

2 tablespoons olive oil

2 tablespoons lemon juice

2 tablespoons water

2 garlic cloves, peeled

½ teaspoon salt

¼ teaspoon black pepper

2 tablespoons grated Parmesan

△ 1½ cups grape tomatoes, halved

1 Preheat oven to 350°F.

2 Place bread crumbs in small baking pan. Bake, stirring once, until lightly toasted, 6–8 minutes. Transfer to plate and let cool.

3 Meanwhile, cook gemelli according to package directions, omitting salt if desired, adding lima beans during last 3 minutes of cooking time. Drain, reserving 1 cup cooking water. Transfer gemelli mixture to large bowl.

4 To make pesto, puree arugula, basil, oil, lemon juice, water, garlic, salt, and pepper in food processor. Stir in Parmesan.

5 Add pesto and tomatoes to gemelli mixture. Toss to coat, adding pasta cooking water, ¼ cup at a time, until mixture is moistened to your liking. Divide among 4 shallow bowls; sprinkle 1 tablespoon bread crumbs over each serving.

Per serving (1½ cups): 374 Cal, 9 g Total Fat, 2 g Sat Fat, 0 g Trans Fat, 2 mg Chol, 680 mg Sod, 62 g Carb, 5 g Sugar, 10 g Fib, 16 g Prot, 126 mg Calc.

miso seitan and broccoli stir-fry

serves 4

- 1 cup brown rice
- 2 tablespoons toasted sesame seeds
- 2 scallions, thinly sliced
- ⅓ cup rice vinegar
- 2 tablespoons white miso
- 1 tablespoon reduced-sodium soy sauce
- 1 teaspoon Asian (dark) sesame oil
- 2 teaspoons canola oil
- 1 pound seitan, drained and cut into 1½-inch pieces
- ¾ pound broccoli, cut into 2-inch florets and stems sliced
- 1 small yellow bell pepper, thinly sliced
- 2 garlic cloves, minced
- 1½ teaspoons grated peeled fresh ginger
- ½ teaspoon red pepper flakes

1 Cook rice according to package directions. Transfer to medium bowl. Stir in sesame seeds and scallions.

2 Meanwhile, whisk together rice vinegar, miso, soy sauce, and sesame oil in small bowl; set aside.

3 Heat canola oil in wok or large skillet over medium-high heat until a drop of water sizzles on pan. Add seitan, broccoli, bell pepper, garlic, ginger, and pepper flakes. Stir-fry until broccoli is crisp-tender, 3–4 minutes. Add vinegar mixture and stir-fry until mixture comes to boil, about 1 minute.

4 Divide rice mixture among 4 plates; top with seitan mixture.

Per serving (1 cup seitan and broccoli and ½ cup rice mixture): 382 Cal, 10 g Total Fat, 1 g Sat Fat, 0 g Trans Fat, 0 mg Chol, 875 mg Sod, 49 g Carb, 3 g Sugar, 9 g Fib, 27 g Prot, 74 mg Calc.

FYI Seitan is made from gluten, the protein found in wheat. It has chewy meat-like texture and can be sautéed, stir-fried, baked, or braised. Look for it in plastic tubs or vacuum-sealed packages in the refrigerated or frozen foods section of health foods stores.

barley and portobello risotto

serves 4

▲ **4 cups reduced-sodium vegetable broth**

1 cup water

2 teaspoons olive oil

▲ **½ pound portobello mushroom caps, gills removed, halved, and sliced**

▲ **2 carrots, chopped**

2 shallots, chopped

2 garlic cloves, minced

▲ **1½ cups pearl barley**

¼ cup grated Parmesan

1 tablespoon butter

1 tablespoon balsamic vinegar

¼ teaspoon salt

2 tablespoons chopped fresh flat-leaf parsley

1 Bring broth and water to boil in medium saucepan. Reduce heat and keep at simmer.

2 Heat oil in large saucepan over medium-high heat. Add mushrooms, carrots, shallots, and garlic. Cook, stirring occasionally, until vegetables are softened, 5 minutes. Add barley and 1 cup broth mixture. Cook, stirring frequently, until broth is absorbed. Add remaining broth mixture, ½ cup at time, stirring until it is absorbed before adding more, until barley is tender, about 25 minutes.

3 Remove from heat. Stir in Parmesan, butter, vinegar, and salt. Spoon into large serving bowl. Sprinkle with parsley and serve at once.

Per serving (1⅓ cups): 390 Cal, 8 g Total Fat, 4 g Sat Fat, 0 g Trans Fat, 12 mg Chol, 756 mg Sod, 70 g Carb, 8 g Sugar, 14 g Fib, 12 g Prot, 137 mg Calc.

FYI The gills on the underside of portobello mushroom caps are edible but will give the risotto a dark color. To remove them, gently scrape them out with a small spoon.

italian vegetable and polenta casserole

serves 6

- ▲ **4 carrots, cut into ½-inch pieces**
- ▲ **2 red bell peppers, cut into ½-inch strips**
- ▲ **1 small butternut squash, peeled, seeded, and cut into ½-inch cubes**
- ▲ **1 red onion, cut into ½-inch wedges**
- ▲ **½ fennel bulb, trimmed and cut into ½-inch strips**
- **2 tablespoons olive oil**
- **½ teaspoon salt**
- **½ teaspoon dried Italian seasoning**
- **¼ teaspoon black pepper**
- ▲ **3 cups fat-free milk**
- **2 cups water**
- ▲ **1½ cups instant polenta**
- **1½ cups shredded reduced-fat Italian cheese blend**
- **⅓ cup chopped fresh basil**

1 Preheat oven to 400°F. Spray large roasting pan with nonstick spray.

2 Place carrots, bell peppers, squash, onion, and fennel in prepared pan. Add oil, salt, Italian seasoning, and pepper; toss to coat. Arrange vegetables in single layer in pan. Roast, stirring once, until vegetables are lightly browned and tender, about 25 minutes. Maintain oven temperature.

3 Meanwhile, combine milk and water in large saucepan; bring to boil over medium-high heat. Slowly pour in polenta in thin, steady stream, whisking constantly. Cook, whisking constantly, until thick and creamy, about 5 minutes. Remove from heat. Stir in 1 cup Italian cheese blend and basil.

4 Spray 9 x 13-inch baking dish with nonstick spray. Spoon polenta into dish and spread evenly. Spoon roasted vegetables evenly over polenta; top with remaining ½ cup cheese. Bake until cheese is melted, about 10 minutes.

Per serving (⅙ of casserole): 355 Cal, 11 g Total Fat, 4 g Sat Fat, 0 g Trans Fat, 18 mg Chol, 774 mg Sod, 50 g Carb, 16 g Sugar, 8 g Fib, 16 g Prot, 546 mg Calc.

nut-crusted eggplant with sundried tomato bulgur

serves 4

- ▲ **1 large eggplant (1½ pounds), cut crosswise into 16 (½-inch-thick) slices**
- **1 tablespoon olive oil**
- **4 tablespoons prepared sundried tomato pesto**
- **½ cup walnuts, chopped**
- **½ teaspoon salt**
- **¼ teaspoon black pepper**
- ▲ **1 cup bulgur**
- ▲ **2 cups reduced-sodium vegetable broth**

1 Preheat oven to 375°F. Spray large rimmed baking sheet with nonstick spray.

2 Brush eggplant slices with oil; then with 2 tablespoons pesto. Arrange eggplant slices in single layer on prepared baking sheet. Sprinkle evenly with walnuts, ¼ teaspoon salt, and pepper. Bake until lightly browned and tender, 18–20 minutes.

3 Meanwhile, combine bulgur, broth, and remaining ¼ teaspoon salt in medium saucepan; bring to boil over high heat. Reduce heat and cover. Simmer until bulgur is tender, about 15 minutes. Remove from heat. Stir in remaining 2 tablespoons pesto. Serve bulgur with eggplant.

Per serving (4 eggplant slices and ½ cup bulgur): 296 Cal, 14 g Total Fat, 2 g Sat Fat, 0 g Trans Fat, 0 mg Chol, 645 mg Sod, 41 g Carb, 6 g Sugar, 13 g Fib, 8 g Prot, 45 mg Calc.

FYI You can use pecans, almonds, or mixed nuts instead of walnuts and basil pesto as a substitute for sundried tomato pesto in this versatile recipe.

squash stuffed with kasha and mushrooms

serves 4

- ½ cup kasha
- 1 large egg, lightly beaten
- 1¼ cups reduced-sodium vegetable broth
- 4 large yellow squash
- ½ cup water
- 2 teaspoons olive oil
- 1 pound mixed mushrooms, coarsely chopped
- 2 shallots, chopped
- 2 scallions, chopped
- 3 garlic cloves, minced
- 1 teaspoon poultry seasoning
- ½ teaspoon salt
- ¼ teaspoon black pepper
- 1 cup shredded reduced-fat mozzarella

1 Place kasha in medium saucepan; stir in egg. Cook over medium heat until mixture becomes dry and groats are separated, about 5 minutes. Stir in broth; bring to boil. Reduce heat and cover. Simmer until kasha is tender and liquid is absorbed, about 15 minutes.

2 Meanwhile, cut each squash in half lengthwise. With small spoon, scoop out and discard most of flesh, leaving ¼ inch of flesh all around. Place squash, cut side down, in microwavable dish. Add water, cover with wax paper, and microwave on High until squash are crisp-tender, 4–5 minutes.

3 Heat oil in large nonstick skillet over medium heat. Add mushrooms, shallots, scallions, and garlic. Cook, stirring occasionally, until vegetables are tender, about 8 minutes. Stir in kasha, poultry seasoning, salt, and pepper.

4 Spoon about ½ cup kasha mixture into each squash half. Return squash to microwavable dish; top evenly with mozzarella. Cover with wax paper and microwave on High until squash are heated through and cheese is melted, 2–3 minutes.

Per serving (2 squash halves): 268 Cal, 11 g Total Fat, 4 g Sat Fat, 0 g Trans Fat, 62 mg Chol, 649 mg Sod, 31 g Carb, 10 g Sugar, 7 g Fib, 19 g Prot, 289 mg Calc.

KABOCHA SQUASH WITH FENNEL STUFFING

kabocha squash with fennel stuffing

serves 4

- ▲ **1 kabocha squash (about 4 pounds)**
- **2 teaspoons olive oil**
- ▲ **1 fennel bulb, cored and chopped**
- ▲ **½ head Savoy cabbage, chopped**
- ▲ **2 large eggs**
- ▲ **1 cup fat-free milk**
- **2 teaspoons minced fresh thyme or ½ teaspoon dried**
- **½ teaspoon salt**
- **¼ teaspoon black pepper**
- **1 cup fresh whole wheat bread crumbs**

1 Preheat oven to 400°F. Line large rimmed baking sheet with foil; spray with nonstick spray.

2 Cut top off squash. Using spoon, scrape out and discard seeds and connective fibers.

3 Heat oil in large skillet over medium heat. Add fennel and cook, stirring occasionally, until softened, 5 minutes. Add cabbage; cook, stirring constantly, until cabbage begins to wilt, about 5 minutes.

4 Whisk together eggs, milk, thyme, salt, and pepper in large bowl. Add fennel mixture and bread crumbs; stir to combine.

5 Spoon mixture into squash; replace top. Place on prepared baking sheet. Bake until squash is tender, 1 hour–1 hour 10 minutes. Let stand 15 minutes. To serve, cut into 4 wedges.

Per serving (¼ of stuffed squash): 217 Cal, 6 g Total Fat, 1 g Sat Fat, 0 g Trans Fat, 94 mg Chol, 474 mg Sod, 34 g Carb, 20 g Sugar, 9 g Fib, 12 g Prot, 215 mg Calc.

CAN'T COMMIT? Add 4 ounces chopped crisp-cooked pancetta to the egg mixture in step 5. The per-serving *PointsPlus* value will increase by **4**.

summer vegetable lasagna

serves 4

2 teaspoons olive oil

2 garlic cloves, minced

▲ 1 (28-ounce) can crushed tomatoes

1 (15-ounce) container part-skim ricotta

▲ 1 large egg white

▲ 1 (16-ounce) package frozen chopped spinach, thawed and squeezed dry

6 (7 x 3-inch) oven-ready no-boil whole wheat lasagna noodles

▲ 2 zucchini, cut lengthwise into thin slices with vegetable peeler

▲ 4 plum tomatoes, sliced

▲ 1 small onion, thinly sliced

1 To make sauce, heat oil in large skillet over medium-high heat. Add garlic and cook, stirring constantly, until fragrant, 1 minute. Add crushed tomatoes. Reduce heat and simmer, stirring occasionally, until sauce is thickened, about 20 minutes.

2 Preheat oven to 400°F. Spray 8-inch square baking dish with nonstick spray.

3 Stir together ricotta and egg white in medium bowl. Stir in spinach.

4 Spread one-third of sauce over bottom of prepared baking dish. Top with 2 lasagna noodles. Layer noodles with half of zucchini, half of ricotta mixture, half of plum tomatoes, half of sliced onion, and one-third of sauce. Repeat layering starting with 2 lasagna noodles and ending with remaining one-third of sauce. Top with remaining 2 lasagna noodles.

5 Cover and bake until bubbling, about 40 minutes. Let stand 10 minutes before serving.

Per serving (¼ of lasagna): 373 Cal, 12 g Total Fat, 6 g Sat Fat, 0 g Trans Fat, 33 mg Chol, 804 mg Sod, 47 g Carb, 16 g Sugar, 10 g Fib, 25 g Prot, 493 mg Calc.

CAN'T COMMIT? Remove the casings and crumble ¼ pound Italian sausage links. Cook with the garlic in step 1, stirring to break up sausage, until no longer pink, 5–7 minutes. Proceed with the recipe. The per-serving *PointsPlus* value will increase by *2*.

shells and broccoli with gorgonzola sauce

serves 4

- ½ pound medium whole wheat pasta shells
- 2 teaspoons olive oil
- 1 onion, chopped
- 2 garlic cloves, minced
- ½ head broccoli, coarsely chopped
- 1 cup reduced-sodium vegetable broth
- ¾ cup part-skim ricotta
- ½ cup fat-free half-and-half
- 2 ounces Gorgonzola, crumbled (⅓ cup)
- ¼ teaspoon black pepper
- ¼ cup fresh basil leaves, torn into small pieces
- 3 plum tomatoes, cut into wedges
- 2 tablespoons grated Asiago

1 Preheat oven to 400°F. Spray 9 x 13-inch baking dish with nonstick spray.

2 Cook pasta according to package directions, omitting salt if desired.

3 Meanwhile, heat oil in large skillet over medium-high heat. Add onion and garlic. Cook, stirring occasionally, until onion is softened, 5 minutes.

4 Add broccoli and broth; bring to boil. Cook, stirring occasionally, until broccoli is tender, 5 minutes. Add pasta, ricotta, half-and-half, Gorgonzola, pepper, and basil. Stir to combine.

5 Spoon into prepared baking dish. Arrange tomatoes evenly over top and sprinkle with Asiago. Bake until tomatoes are heated through and cheese is melted, about 15 minutes.

Per serving (¼ of casserole): 411 Cal, 13 g Total Fat, 7 g Sat Fat, 0 g Trans Fat, 30 mg Chol, 693 mg Sod, 58 g Carb, 8 g Sugar, 7 g Fib, 21 g Prot, 333 mg Calc.

**GREEK SPINACH AND FETA
LASAGNA**

greek spinach and feta lasagna

serves 8

- 1 (15-ounce) container fat-free ricotta cheese
- 1 (10-ounce) package frozen chopped spinach, thawed and squeezed dry
- 2 cups shredded fat-free mozzarella cheese
- 4 ounces crumbled reduced-fat feta cheese (about 1 cup)
- 8 kalamata olives, pitted and coarsely chopped
- 1 large egg, lightly beaten
- 1 teaspoon dried oregano
- 1 (24-ounce) jar fat-free tomato-basil marinara sauce
- 9 oven-ready no-boil lasagna noodles

1 Preheat oven to 375°F. Spray 9 x 13-inch baking dish with nonstick spray.

2 Combine ricotta cheese, spinach, 1 cup mozzarella cheese, feta cheese, olives, egg, and oregano in large bowl; mix well.

3 Spread one-fourth (about ¾ cup) of tomato sauce over bottom of baking dish. Top with 3 lasagna noodles. Spread half (about 2 cups) of ricotta mixture over noodles. Spread with one-fourth more tomato sauce. Repeat layering once more with 3 noodles, remaining half of ricotta mixture, and one-fourth more tomato sauce. Top with the remaining 3 noodles, one-fourth sauce, and 1 cup mozzarella cheese.

4 Lightly spray sheet of foil with nonstick spray; cover baking dish with foil, sprayed side down and bake 30 minutes. Uncover and bake until cheese melts and lasagna is heated through and bubbling, 10–15 minutes longer.

Per serving (⅛ of lasagna): 236 Cal, 4 g Total Fat, 2 g Sat Fat, 0 g Trans Fat, 67 mg Chol, 982 mg Sod, 28 g Carb, 11 g Sugar, 3 g Fib, 22 g Prot, 472 mg Calc.

pappardelle with sherried mushrooms

serves 4

- ▲ ½ **pound whole wheat pappardelle or fettuccine**
- **1 tablespoon olive oil**
- ▲ ¾ **pound mixed mushrooms, sliced**
- **5 garlic cloves, minced**
- **2 tablespoons dry sherry**
- **½ teaspoon salt**
- **⅛ teaspoon black pepper**
- **⅛ teaspoon ground nutmeg**
- **½ cup chopped fresh flat-leaf parsley**
- **1 tablespoon grated lemon zest**

1 Cook pasta according to package directions, omitting salt if desired. Drain, reserving 1 cup cooking water.

2 Meanwhile, heat oil in large skillet over medium-high heat. Add mushrooms and 3 cloves garlic. Cook, stirring occasionally, until mushrooms are softened, about 5 minutes. Add sherry, salt, pepper, and nutmeg. Cook, stirring constantly, until most of liquid evaporates, 1 minute.

3 Transfer pasta and mushroom mixture to large bowl. Add ½ cup pasta cooking water and toss to coat. Add remaining pasta cooking water, a few tablespoons at a time, if mixture seems dry.

4 Stir together parsley, remaining 2 cloves garlic, and lemon zest in small bowl. Sprinkle over pasta and serve at once.

Per serving (1½ cups): 263 Cal, 5 g Total Fat, 1 g Sat Fat, 0 g Trans Fat, 0 mg Chol, 533 mg Sod, 49 g Carb, 3 g Sugar, 7 g Fib, 11 g Prot, 48 mg Calc.

FYI Different varieties of mushrooms have different flavors and textures, which will add interest to this dish. If your supermarket doesn't sell loose mushrooms, look for prepackaged variety packs with several types of mushrooms in one package.

eggplant with fontina stuffing

serves 4

▲ **2 small eggplants**

4 teaspoons olive oil

2 shallots, thinly sliced

4 sun-dried tomatoes (not oil-packed), diced

▲ **2 plum tomatoes, diced**

2 ounces fontina cheese, shredded

1 teaspoon fresh thyme or ½ teaspoon dried

½ teaspoon salt

⅛ teaspoon black pepper

1 cup fresh whole wheat bread crumbs

1 tablespoon Dijon mustard

1 Preheat oven to 375°F. Spray medium rimmed baking sheet with nonstick spray.

2 Cut eggplants in half lengthwise. With small spoon or melon baller, scoop out most of flesh, leaving ½-inch border all around. Chop flesh.

3 Heat 2 teaspoons oil in medium nonstick skillet over medium heat. Add shallots and cook, stirring often, until softened, 3 minutes. Add chopped eggplant; cook, stirring often, until tender, 8 minutes. Transfer to large bowl. Stir in sun-dried tomatoes, plum tomatoes, fontina, thyme, salt, and pepper.

4 Wipe out skillet. Add remaining 2 teaspoons oil to skillet. Add bread crumbs and cook, stirring often, until toasted, 5 minutes. Transfer to small bowl; stir in mustard.

5 Mound eggplant mixture into eggplant halves; top evenly with bread crumb mixture. Place on prepared baking sheet; cover loosely with foil. Bake until eggplant halves are tender, about 30 minutes.

6 Remove baking sheet from oven. Increase oven temperature to broil. Remove foil and broil 5 inches from heat until bread crumbs are browned and crisp, 1–2 minutes.

Per serving (½ stuffed eggplant): 199 Cal, 10 g Total Fat, 4 g Sat Fat, 0 g Trans Fat, 16 mg Chol, 636 mg Sod, 22 g Carb, 8 g Sugar, 9 g Fib, 8 g Prot, 123 mg Calc.

CAN'T COMMIT? Add 4 ounces minced prosciutto when you add the tomatoes in step 3. The per-serving **PointsPlus** value will increase by **3**.

gnocchi with asparagus, peas, and tomatoes

serves 4 ready in 20 minutes or less

1 (17½-ounce) package refrigerated whole wheat gnocchi

▲ 1 pound asparagus, trimmed and cut into 1-inch pieces

1 tablespoon olive oil

▲ ½ sweet onion, chopped

4 garlic cloves, minced

▲ 4 tomatoes, seeded and chopped

▲ 1 cup frozen green peas, thawed

¼ teaspoon salt

⅛ teaspoon black pepper

¼ cup thinly sliced fresh basil

2 tablespoons shaved Parmesan

1 Cook gnocchi according to package directions, omitting salt if desired, adding asparagus during last 3 minutes of cooking time. Drain, reserving 1 cup cooking water.

2 Meanwhile, heat oil in large nonstick skillet over medium heat. Add onion and garlic. Cook, stirring often, until onion is softened, 5 minutes. Add tomatoes, peas, salt, and pepper. Cook, stirring often, until heated through, about 5 minutes.

3 Add gnocchi mixture and pasta cooking water to skillet. Cook, stirring constantly, until heated through, 3 minutes. Remove from heat. Stir in basil and sprinkle with cheese.

Per serving (1½ cups): 324 Cal, 6 g Total Fat, 1 g Sat Fat, 0 g Trans Fat, 2 mg Chol, 874 mg Sod, 60 g Carb, 6 g Sugar, 8 g Fib, 11 g Prot, 110 mg Calc.

CAN'T COMMIT? Cut 4 ounces of prosciutto into thin strips and stir in along with the gnocchi in step 3. The per-serving *PointsPlus* value will increase by *3*.

creamy penne primavera

serves 4

- 1 cup reduced-sodium vegetable broth
- ½ cup fat-free half-and-half
- ½ pound whole wheat penne

  2 teaspoons olive oil
- ½ pound asparagus, trimmed and cut into 1-inch pieces
- 2 zucchini, cut into matchstick strips
- 2 (4-ounce) packages assorted fresh wild mushrooms (such as oyster, crimini, and shiitake), sliced (remove stems if using shiitakes)
- 1 cup shelled fresh or frozen green peas

  2 tablespoons grated Parmesan cheese

1 Combine broth and half-and-half in small saucepan; set over medium heat. Cook until mixture is reduced by half, about 10 minutes. Set aside.

2 Meanwhile, cook pasta according to package instructions, omitting salt if desired.

3 Heat oil in large nonstick skillet over medium heat. Add asparagus, zucchini, mushrooms, and peas. Cook, stirring often, until vegetables are crisp-tender, about 6 minutes. Add pasta and broth mixture. Cook, stirring often, until heated through, about 1 minute.

4 Divide pasta among 4 plates; sprinkle evenly with Parmesan.

Per serving (1½ cups pasta mixture and ½ tablespoon cheese): 316 Cal, 5 g Total Fat, 1 g Sat Fat, 0 g Trans Fat, 4 mg Chol, 446 mg Sod, 57 g Carb, 10 g Sugar, 9 g Fib, 16 g Prot, 134 mg Calc.

CANT' COMMIT? Add 4 ounces cubed reduced-sodium lean ham when you add the pasta in step 3. The per-serving **PointsPlus** will increase by **1**.

fettuccine with zucchini ribbons and tomatoes

serves 4

▲ ½ pound whole wheat fettuccine
▲ 3 large zucchini
  1 teaspoon olive oil
▲ 1 large onion, sliced
  2 garlic cloves, minced
  ⅛–¼ teaspoon red pepper flakes
▲ 4 plum tomatoes, chopped
  ½ teaspoon salt
  ⅛ teaspoon black pepper
  4 tablespoons grated Parmesan

1 Cook pasta according to package directions, omitting salt if desired. Keep warm.

2 Meanwhile, using vegetable peeler, cut zucchini into thin lengthwise slices. Set aside.

3 Heat oil in large skillet over medium-high heat. Add onion, garlic, and pepper flakes. Cook, stirring occasionally, until onion is softened, 5 minutes.

4 Add tomatoes, salt, and black pepper; cook, stirring occasionally, until tomatoes are softened, 5 minutes. Add zucchini and cook, stirring often, just until zucchini is heated through, about 3 minutes. Add pasta and toss to combine.

5 Divide pasta mixture among 4 plates; sprinkle evenly with Parmesan.

Per serving (1½ cups pasta with 1 tablespoon cheese): 304 Cal, 5 g Total Fat, 2 g Sat Fat, 0 g Trans Fat, 5 mg Chol, 659 mg Sod, 56 g Carb, 10 g Sugar, 8 g Fib, 15 g Prot, 164 mg Calc.

CAN'T COMMIT? Remove the casings and crumble ¼ pound sweet Italian-style sausage links. Cook with the onion mixture in step 3. The per-serving *PointsPlus* value will increase by **2**.

eggplant and olive stew

serves 4

1 tablespoon canola oil

▲ 2 onions, sliced

4 garlic cloves, minced

2¾ cups water

▲ 1 (14½-ounce) can diced tomatoes

1 teaspoon paprika

½ teaspoon salt

½ teaspoon ground ginger

½ teaspoon ground cumin

▲ 1 eggplant (about 1½ pounds), cut into 1-inch cubes

½ cup pitted green olives, coarsely chopped

2 tablespoons golden raisins

▲ 1 cup bulgur

Lemon wedges

1 Heat oil in large saucepan over medium-high heat. Add onions and garlic. Cook, stirring occasionally, until onions are softened, about 5 minutes. Add ¾ cup water, tomatoes, paprika, salt, ginger, and cumin. Bring to boil. Add eggplant, olives, and raisins. Reduce heat and cover. Simmer, stirring occasionally, until eggplant is tender, about 25 minutes.

2 Meanwhile, combine bulgur and remaining 2 cups water in medium saucepan; bring to boil over high heat. Reduce heat and cover. Simmer until bulgur is tender, about 15 minutes.

3 Divide bulgur among 4 bowls; ladle stew evenly over bulgur. Serve with lemon wedges.

Per serving (1½ cups stew and ½ cup bulgur): 293 Cal, 7 g Total Fat, 1 g Sat Fat, 0 g Trans Fat, 0 mg Chol, 746 mg Sod, 56 g Carb, 14 g Sugar, 13 g Fib, 8 g Prot, 93 mg Calc.

CAN'T COMMIT? Cook ½ pound ground skinless turkey breast with the onions and garlic in step 1. The per-serving *PointsPlus* value will increase by *2*.

green curry vegetables with quinoa

serves 4

- ¾ cup red quinoa
- 4 cups reduced-sodium vegetable broth
- 2 tablespoons Thai green curry paste
- 2 teaspoons chili-garlic paste
- 3 small Japanese eggplants, cut into 1-inch-thick slices
- 1 red bell pepper, chopped
- 1 small red onion, thinly sliced
- ¾ pound green beans, trimmed and cut into 1-inch pieces
- 1 (10-ounce) package frozen corn kernels
- 4 (½-inch) strips lime zest, removed with vegetable peeler
- 12 basil leaves, thinly sliced
- 12 mint leaves, thinly sliced

1 Prepare quinoa according to package directions.

2 Meanwhile, bring broth to boil in large saucepan over medium-high heat. Add curry paste and chili-garlic paste, stirring until curry paste dissolves.

3 Add eggplants, bell pepper, onion, green beans, corn, and lime zest; return to boil. Reduce heat and cover. Simmer until vegetables are tender, about 5 minutes.

4 Remove from heat. Stir in basil and mint. Remove and discard lime zest. Spoon quinoa into 4 bowls; top evenly with curry.

Per serving (1 cup curry and ⅓ cup quinoa): 264 Cal, 3 g Total Fat, 0 g Sat Fat, 0 g Trans Fat, 0 mg Chol, 874 mg Sod, 52 g Carb, 11 g Sugar, 11 g Fib, 13 g Prot, 88 mg Calc.

CAN'T COMMIT? Add ½ pound skinless boneless chicken breasts, cut into thin strips along with the eggplants in step 3. Cook until chicken is no longer pink, 5–8 minutes. The per-serving *PointsPlus* value will increase by *1*.

grilled pizza with gouda and kale

serves 4

3 teaspoons olive oil

▲ 1 (12-ounce) bunch lacinato kale, tough stems removed, leaves left whole

▲ 1 large red onion, cut into ¼-inch slices

1 pound refrigerated or thawed frozen pizza dough

▲ 2 large beefsteak tomatoes, cut into ¼-inch slices

½ cup shredded Gouda

1 Brush grill rack with 1 teaspoon oil. Preheat grill to medium-high or prepare medium-hot fire.

2 Brush kale and onion with remaining 2 teaspoons oil. Place on grill rack. Grill, turning often, until vegetables are lightly browned and crisp-tender, 3 minutes. Maintain grill temperature. Transfer vegetables to cutting board and coarsely chop.

3 On lightly floured surface, roll dough into 12-inch circle. Lightly spray dough with olive oil nonstick spray on both sides. Place dough on grill rack and grill until browned on underside, about 3 minutes. Remove crust from grill.

4 Top browned side of crust with kale, onions, tomatoes, and Gouda. Return pizza to grill rack and grill until underside is browned and cheese is melted, about 3 minutes.

Per serving (¼ of pizza): 421 Cal, 14 g Total Fat, 4 g Sat Fat, 0 g Trans Fat, 16 mg Chol, 619 mg Sod, 62 g Carb, 6 g Sugar, 5 g Fib, 13 g Prot, 198 mg Calc.

CAN'T COMMIT? Add ¼ pound diced skinless smoked duck breast to the pizza when you add the kale in step 4. The per-serving *PointsPlus* value will increase by *2*.

chapter 4
tastes like chicken

tofu parmesan

serves 4

- **2 teaspoons olive oil**
- ▲ **1 small onion, chopped**
- **2 garlic cloves, minced**
- ▲ **1 (14½-ounce) can diced tomatoes with basil, garlic, and oregano**
- **1 tablespoon tomato paste**
- ▲ **2 egg whites**
- **⅓ cup Italian-seasoned dried bread crumbs**
- **1 tablespoon grated Parmesan cheese**
- ▲ **1½ (14-ounce) packages firm tofu, drained and cut into 8 slices**
- **½ cup shredded part-skim mozzarella**

1 Spray 9 x 13-inch flameproof baking dish with nonstick spray.

2 To make sauce, heat 1 teaspoon oil in medium saucepan over medium heat. Add onion; cover and cook, stirring occasionally, until softened, 5 minutes. Add garlic; cook, stirring constantly, until fragrant, 1 minute. Add tomatoes and tomato paste; bring to boil. Reduce heat and cover. Simmer until vegetables are tender, 6–8 minutes.

3 Meanwhile, beat egg whites in shallow bowl. Combine bread crumbs and Parmesan on sheet of wax paper. Dip each slice tofu into egg whites, then into bread crumb mixture, turning to coat evenly. Discard any leftover egg whites and bread crumb mixture.

4 Preheat broiler.

5 Heat remaining 1 teaspoon oil in large nonstick skillet over medium heat. Add tofu and cook, turning once, until lightly browned, 10–12 minutes. Place tofu in single layer in prepared baking dish.

6 Top tofu with tomato sauce; sprinkle evenly with mozzarella. Broil 5 inches from heat until cheese is melted, about 2 minutes.

Per serving (2 slices tofu and ½ cup sauce): 246 Cal, 12 g Total Fat, 4 g Sat Fat, 0 g Trans Fat, 9 mg Chol, 408 mg Sod, 16 g Carb, 5 g Sugar, 3 g Fib, 21 g Prot, 485 mg Calc.

seitan and bell pepper stir-fry

serves 4

3 teaspoons canola oil

▲ 1 small red onion, sliced

2 teaspoons grated peeled fresh ginger

▲ 1 (20-ounce) can pineapple chunks in juice, drained and juice reserved

▲ 3 assorted-color bell peppers, chopped

2 tablespoons brown sugar

2 tablespoons ketchup

2 tablespoons white-wine vinegar

2 tablespoons reduced-sodium soy sauce

2 tablespoons water

2 teaspoons cornstarch

1 pound seitan, drained and thinly sliced

1 To make sauce, heat 1 teaspoon oil in medium saucepan over medium heat. Add onion and ginger; cook, stirring often, until onion is softened, 5 minutes. Add pineapple juice, bell peppers, brown sugar, ketchup, vinegar, and soy sauce; bring to boil. Reduce heat and cover. Simmer until vegetables are tender, 10 minutes. Stir in pineapple chunks.

2 Whisk together water and cornstarch in small bowl; add mixture to saucepan. Cook, stirring constantly, until mixture comes to boil and thickens, 1 minute.

3 Meanwhile, heat remaining 2 teaspoons oil in large nonstick skillet over medium heat. Add seitan and cook, stirring often, until lightly browned, 2–3 minutes.

4 Divide seitan among 4 plates; top evenly with sauce.

Per serving (¼ of seitan and 1 cup sauce): 323 Cal, 5 g Total Fat, 0 g Sat Fat, 0 g Trans Fat, 0 mg Chol, 738 mg Sod, 53 g Carb, 33 g Sugar, 4 g Fib, 20 g Prot, 42 mg Calc.

bbq tofu

serves 4

- ▲ 1 orange
- 1 teaspoon canola oil
- ▲ 1 small onion, minced
- ¼ cup tomato paste
- ⅓ cup water
- 2 tablespoons white vinegar
- 2 teaspoons light brown sugar
- ¼ teaspoon salt
- ¼ teaspoon ground allspice
- Pinch ground cloves
- Pinch cayenne
- ▲ 1½ (14-ounce) packages extra-firm tofu, drained and cut into 8 slices

1 To make sauce, grate zest from orange and set aside. Peel orange and cut between the membranes to release segments over small bowl.

2 Heat oil in medium saucepan over medium-high heat. Add onion and cook, stirring occasionally, until softened, 5 minutes. Add tomato paste and cook, stirring constantly, 1 minute. Pour any juice from orange segments into saucepan; reserve segments. Stir in water, vinegar, brown sugar, salt, allspice, cloves, cayenne, and orange zest; bring to boil. Reduce heat and simmer, partially covered, until sauce is thickened, about 20 minutes.

3 Meanwhile, preheat oven to 350°F. Spray 9 x 13-inch baking dish with nonstick spray.

4 Arrange tofu in single layer in prepared dish. Pour sauce over tofu; top with orange segments. Bake until tofu is heated through, about 20 minutes.

Per serving (2 slices tofu with 3 tablespoons sauce): 193 Cal, 10 g Total Fat, 1 g Sat Fat, 0 g Trans Fat, 0 mg Chol, 292 mg Sod, 14 g Carb, 8 g Sugar, 2 g Fib, 16 g Prot, 289 mg Calc.

STAY ON TRACK To make a quick side dish to serve with the tofu, thinly slice 1 red bell pepper, 1 green bell pepper, and 1 onion. Spray a large nonstick skillet with nonstick spray and set over medium heat. Add the vegetables and cook, stirring often, until crisp-tender, about 8 minutes

CLOCKWISE FROM TOP:
BBQ TOFU,
TOFU LETTUCE WRAPS
WITH PEANUT SAUCE,
PAGE 152, AND MOO SHU
TOFU AND VEGETABLES,
PAGE 140

moo shu tofu and vegetables

serves 4

1 teaspoon canola oil

▲ 3 shitake mushrooms, stems removed and caps thinly sliced

▲ 2 scallions, thinly sliced

▲ 1 small bok choy, thinly sliced

▲ 1 carrot, cut into matchstick strips

1 teaspoon grated peeled fresh ginger

2 tablespoons water

4 teaspoons black bean sauce

1 teaspoon cornstarch

▲ 1 (14-ounce) package firm tofu, drained and cut into ½-inch cubes

4 (8-inch) whole wheat tortillas, warmed

4 teaspoons hoisin sauce

1 Heat oil in large nonstick skillet over medium heat. Add mushrooms and cook, stirring occasionally, until softened, 3 minutes. Add scallions, bok choy, carrot, and ginger. Cook, stirring occasionally, until vegetables are crisp-tender, 6–8 minutes.

2 Stir together water, black bean sauce, and cornstarch in small bowl. Add tofu and black bean mixture to skillet. Cook stirring often, until tofu is heated through and sauce thickens, about 5 minutes.

3 Spread each tortilla with 1 teaspoon hoisin sauce. Top with about ¾ cup tofu mixture and roll up to enclose filling.

Per serving (1 filled tortilla): 225 Cal, 8 g Total Fat, 1 g Sat Fat, 0 g Trans Fat, 0 mg Chol, 453 mg Sod, 30 g Carb, 4 g Sugar, 6 g Fib, 15 g Prot, 399 mg Calc.

FYI Asian black bean sauce is made from soybeans that have been fermented and cooked with garlic, soy sauce, and rice vinegar. It adds a pungent salty flavor to many Chinese dishes.

roasted tofu and vegetables

serves 4

2 tablespoons balsamic vinegar

2 tablespoons white grape juice or orange juice

1 garlic clove, minced

½ teaspoon chopped fresh oregano

▲ 1½ (14-ounce) packages extra-firm tofu, drained and cut into 8 slices

▲ ½ sweet onion, sliced

▲ 1 green bell pepper, sliced

▲ 1 red bell pepper, sliced

1 teaspoon olive oil

⅛ teaspoon salt

¼ teaspoon black pepper

1 Preheat oven to 425°F. Spray large rimmed baking sheet with cooking spray.

2 Stir together vinegar, grape juice, garlic, and oregano in 9 x 13-inch baking dish. Add tofu and turn to coat. Cover and refrigerate 20 minutes.

3 Meanwhile, place onion and bell peppers on prepared baking sheet. Drizzle with oil and sprinkle with salt and black pepper. Toss to coat. Roast vegetables 20 minutes. Remove pan from oven. Stir vegetables and push to one side of baking sheet.

4 Drain tofu, reserving marinade. Arrange tofu in single layer on baking sheet. Roast until vegetables are tender and slightly browned and tofu is heated through, about 15 minutes. Stir vegetables, drizzle tofu with reserved marinade, and roast 5 minutes longer.

Per serving (2 slices tofu and ½ cup vegetables): 179 Cal, 10 g Total Fat, 1 g Sat Fat, 0 g Trans Fat, 0 mg Chol, 238 mg Sod, 10 g Carb, 5 g Sugar, 2 g Fib, 16 g Prot, 274 mg Calc.

STAY ON TRACK Quinoa makes an easy and flavorful side dish for the tofu and vegetables; ½ cup of cooked quinoa per serving will increase the *PointsPlus* value by *3*.

moroccan vegetable stew with couscous

serves 4

2 teaspoons canola oil

▲ 1 small onion, chopped

¼ teaspoon turmeric

⅛ teaspoon ground ginger

Pinch saffron

▲ 2 cups reduced-sodium vegetable broth

▲ 3 carrots, thickly sliced

▲ 1 tomato, chopped

▲ ½ cauliflower, cut into florets

1 (3-inch) stick cinnamon

¼ teaspoon salt

▲ 2 zucchini, halved lengthwise and thickly sliced

▲ 1 small butternut squash, peeled, seeded, and cut into 1-inch pieces

▲ 1 cup whole wheat couscous

2 tablespoons golden raisins

2 tablespoons sliced almonds

Chopped fresh cilantro (optional)

1 Heat oil in large saucepan over medium heat. Add onion and cook, stirring occasionally, until softened, 5 minutes. Add turmeric, ginger, and saffron; cook, stirring constantly, until fragrant, 1 minute. Add broth, carrots, tomato, cauliflower, cinnamon stick, and salt; bring to boil. Reduce heat and cover. Simmer 10 minutes.

2 Stir in zucchini and squash. Cover and simmer until vegetables are tender, 8–10 minutes. Uncover and simmer until liquid is slightly reduced, 5 minutes. Remove and discard cinnamon stick.

3 Meanwhile, prepare couscous according to package directions. Divide couscous among 4 bowls; top evenly with stew. Sprinkle evenly with raisins, almonds, and cilantro, if using.

Per serving (1½ cups stew, ¾ cup couscous, and ½ tablespoon each raisins and almonds): 355 Cal, 5 g Total Fat, 0 g Sat Fat, 0 g Trans Fat, 0 mg Chol, 438 mg Sod, 70 g Carb, 21 g Sugar, 15 g Fib, 12 g Prot, 151 mg Calc.

red lentil and coconut stew

serves 6

2 cups water

1 (14-ounce) can light (reduced-fat) coconut milk

1 tablespoon canola oil

▲ 2 onions, finely chopped

1 tablespoon minced peeled fresh ginger

4 garlic cloves, peeled

1 teaspoon ground coriander

¾ teaspoon ground cumin

½ teaspoon salt

¼ teaspoon ground cardamom

¼ teaspoon red pepper flakes

▲ 1 pound red lentils, picked over and rinsed

▲ 2 cups reduced-sodium vegetable broth

▲ 4 carrots, finely chopped

▲ 1 (10-ounce) package frozen green peas, thawed

1¼ cups fresh cilantro leaves

1 Whisk together water and coconut milk in medium bowl.

2 Heat oil in large nonstick skillet over medium heat. Add onions and cook, stirring frequently, until softened and lightly browned, 5 minutes. Stir in ginger, garlic, coriander, cumin, salt, cardamom, and pepper flakes. Cook, stirring constantly, until fragrant, about 30 seconds. Transfer to 5- or 6-quart slow cooker.

3 Stir in coconut milk mixture, lentils, broth, and carrots. Cover and cook 4–6 hours on high or 8–10 hours on low. Stir in peas; cover and cook on high 5 minutes. Stir in cilantro just before serving.

Per serving (1⅔ cups): 371 Cal, 7 g Total Fat, 2 g Sat Fat, 0 g Trans Fat, 0 mg Chol, 420 mg Sod, 59 g Carb, 8 g Sugar, 16 g Fib, 23 g Prot, 84 mg Calc.

lentil and vegetable stew with mint

serves 6

1 tablespoon olive oil

2 small leeks, cleaned and thinly sliced, white and light green parts only

3 garlic cloves, minced

4 cups reduced-sodium vegetable broth, heated

1½ cups green or brown lentils

4 celery stalks including leaves, finely chopped

3 small carrots, finely chopped

2 small turnips, peeled and finely chopped

6 tablespoons apple cider vinegar

3 tablespoons brown sugar

2 bay leaves

½ teaspoon salt

¼ teaspoon black pepper

¼ cup thinly sliced fresh mint leaves

3 tablespoons toasted pumpkin seeds (pepitas)

1 Heat oil in medium nonstick skillet over medium heat. Add leeks and cook, stirring frequently, until softened, about 3 minutes. Stir in garlic and cook, stirring constantly, until fragrant, about 30 seconds. Transfer to 5- or 6-quart slow cooker.

2 Stir in hot broth, lentils, celery, carrots, turnips, vinegar, brown sugar, bay leaves, salt, and pepper. Cover and cook 4–6 hours on high or 8–10 hours on low. Remove and discard bay leaves. Stir in mint just before serving. Ladle stew into 6 bowls; sprinkle evenly with pumpkin seeds.

Per serving (generous 1 cup stew and ½ tablespoon pumpkin seeds): 265 Cal, 5 g Total Fat, 1 g Sat Fat, 0 g Trans Fat, 0 mg Chol, 536 mg Sod, 44 g Carb, 14 g Sugar, 10 g Fib, 14 g Prot, 80 mg Calc.

CAN'T COMMIT? The meaty, salty taste of Canadian bacon is a terrific counterpoint to the sweet-and-sour lentils. If you wish, you can stir in 4 slices Canadian bacon, cut into thin strips, along with the mint. The per-serving **PointsPlus** value will increase by **1**.

wheat berry and summer vegetable stew

serves 4

1 tablespoon olive oil

▲ 2 leeks, cleaned and sliced, white and light green parts only

▲ ¾ cup finely chopped fennel bulb

2 garlic cloves, minced

▲ 1 cup wheat berries

▲ 2½ cups reduced-sodium vegetable broth, heated

1 large sprig fresh basil plus ¼ cup thinly sliced fresh basil

½ teaspoon salt

¼ teaspoon black pepper

▲ 2 zucchini, halved lengthwise and sliced

▲ ¼ pound green beans, cut into 1½-inch lengths

▲ 1 (10-ounce) package grape or cherry tomatoes, quartered

1 Heat oil in medium nonstick skillet over medium heat. Add leeks and cook, stirring frequently, until softened, about 3 minutes. Add fennel and garlic; cook, stirring constantly, until fragrant, about 30 seconds. Add wheat berries and stir to coat. Transfer to 3- or 4-quart slow cooker.

2 Stir in hot broth, basil sprig, salt, and pepper. Cover and cook 5 hours on high. Stir in zucchini and green beans. Cover and cook on high 1 hour. Discard basil sprig. Stir in grape tomatoes and sliced basil just before serving.

Per serving (1¼ cups): 254 Cal, 5 g Total Fat, 1 g Sat Fat, 0 g Trans Fat, 0 mg Chol, 596 mg Sod, 50 g Carb, 11 g Sugar, 8 g Fib, 8 g Prot, 99 mg Calc.

FYI When cooking wheat berries in a slow cooker, it helps the grains to cook faster and more evenly if the added cooking liquid is heated first.

many mushroom stew with egg noodles

serves 4

1 tablespoon olive oil

▲ 1 large red onion, quartered and thinly sliced

4 garlic cloves, minced

▲ 1½ pounds assorted fresh mushrooms (such as white, oyster, cremini, and shiitake), thinly sliced (remove stems if using shiitakes)

1 teaspoon reduced-sodium soy sauce

¼ teaspoon salt

¼ teaspoon black pepper

▲ 2 cups whole wheat egg noodles

▲ 1 (14½-ounce) can petite diced tomatoes, drained

3 tablespoons chopped fresh flat-leaf parsley

1 teaspoon grated lemon zest

2 tablespoons shaved Parmesan cheese

1 Heat oil in large deep nonstick skillet over medium heat. Add onion and cook, stirring constantly, until softened, 5 minutes. Add garlic and cook, stirring constantly, until fragrant, about 30 seconds. Add mushrooms and cook, stirring frequently, until mushrooms release their liquid and it evaporates, about 15 minutes. Transfer to 3- or 4-quart slow cooker. Stir in soy sauce, salt, and pepper. Cover and cook 2 hours on high or 4 hours on low.

2 About 15 minutes before end of cooking time, prepare noodles according to package directions.

3 Stir in tomatoes. Cover and cook on high heat until heated through, 5 minutes. Stir in parsley and lemon zest just before serving. Divide egg noodles among 4 bowls; top evenly with stew. Sprinkle with Parmesan.

Per serving (¾ cup stew, ½ cup noodles, and ½ tablespoon cheese): 197 Cal, 6 g Total Fat, 1 g Sat Fat, 0 g Trans Fat, 18 mg Chol, 426 mg Sod, 32 g Carb, 7 g Sugar, 6 g Fib, 11 g Prot, 102 mg Calc.

STAY ON TRACK Serve a green vegetable as a side dish with this meal. Drizzle steamed green beans with lemon juice and sprinkle with salt and pepper to taste.

indian-spiced vegetable stew

serves 6

- 1 tablespoon canola oil
- 1 large red onion, thinly sliced
- 3 garlic cloves, minced
- 2 teaspoons minced peeled fresh ginger
- 1½ teaspoons ground coriander
- 1 teaspoon cumin seeds
- ¼ teaspoon ground turmeric
- 6 cups 1- to 1½-inch cauliflower florets
- 3 small red potatoes (¾ pound), cut into ½-inch cubes
- 1 cup reduced-sodium vegetable broth
- 1 (8-ounce) can tomato sauce
- ½ teaspoon salt
- ⅛ teaspoon cayenne
- ¼ pound green beans, cut into 1½-inch lengths
- 1½ cups fresh cilantro leaves
- 3 cups cooked brown basmati rice

1 Heat oil in large nonstick skillet over medium heat. Add onion, and cook, stirring frequently, until softened, about 5 minutes. Add garlic, ginger, coriander, cumin seeds, and turmeric. Cook, stirring constantly, until fragrant, about 30 seconds. Transfer to 3- or 4-quart slow cooker.

2 Stir in cauliflower, potatoes, broth, tomato sauce, salt, and cayenne. Cover and cook 3 hours on high or 6 hours on low. About 30 minutes before end of cooking time, stir in green beans. Stir in cilantro just before serving. Serve with brown rice.

Per serving (1⅓ cup stew and ½ cup rice): 246 Cal, 4 g Total Fat, 0 g Sat Fat, 0 g Trans Fat, 0 mg Chol, 495 mg Sod, 48 g Carb, 6 g Sugar, 9 g Fib, 7 g Prot, 73 mg Calc.

CAN'T COMMIT? Add ¾ pound skinless boneless chicken thighs, cut into ½-inch pieces, along with the cauliflower in step 2. The per-serving **PointsPlus** value will increase by **3**.

paneer and bell pepper curry

serves 4

1 tablespoon canola oil

6 ounces reduced-fat paneer, cut into ½-inch cubes

▲ 2 medium red onions, thinly sliced

3 garlic cloves, minced

2 teaspoons minced peeled fresh ginger

1½ teaspoons garam masala

1½ teaspoons cumin seeds

½ teaspoon salt

⅛ teaspoon cayenne

▲ 6 medium yellow bell peppers, thinly sliced

▲ 1 (14½-ounce) can diced tomatoes

1 cup fresh cilantro leaves

▲ 2 cups cooked brown rice

1 Heat oil in large nonstick skillet over medium heat. Add paneer and cook, stirring frequently, until browned, about 6 minutes. Transfer paneer to 5- or 6-quart slow cooker.

2 Add onions to same skillet and cook, stirring frequently, until softened, about 5 minutes. Add garlic, ginger, garam masala, cumin seeds, salt, and cayenne. Cook, stirring constantly, until fragrant, about 30 seconds. Transfer to slow cooker.

3 Stir in bell peppers and tomatoes. Cover and cook 4–6 hours on high or 8–10 hours on low. Stir in cilantro just before serving. Serve with brown rice.

Per serving (1¼ cups curry and ½ cup rice): 337 Cal, 12 g Total Fat, 5 g Sat Fat, 0 g Trans Fat, 24 mg Chol, 683 mg Sod, 47 g Carb, 16 g Sugar, 7 g Fib, 16 g Prot, 244 mg Calc.

FYI Paneer is a fresh cow's milk cheese used in Indian cuisine. It has a firm texture and mild flavor. Look for it in specialty supermarkets.

PANEER AND BELL PEPPER CURRY

buckwheat stew with tofu and kale

serves 4

1 tablespoon olive oil

▲ 2 red onions, finely chopped

2 garlic cloves, minced

▲ 3 cups reduced-sodium vegetable broth

▲ 1 cup raw whole buckwheat groats (not kasha)

▲ ½ pound firm tofu, cut into ½-inch cubes

▲ 2 celery stalks including leaves, finely chopped

2 teaspoons reduced-sodium soy sauce

¼ teaspoon black pepper

▲ 2 cups thinly sliced kale

½ cup chopped fresh cilantro

¾ teaspoon Asian (dark) sesame oil

1 Heat olive oil in large nonstick skillet over medium heat. Add onions and cook, stirring frequently, until softened, 5 minutes. Add garlic and cook, stirring constantly, until fragrant, about 30 seconds. Transfer to 3- or 4-quart slow cooker.

2 Stir in broth, buckwheat, tofu, celery, soy sauce, and pepper. Cover and cook 4–6 hours on high or 8–10 hours on low. About 30 minutes before end of cooking time, stir in kale. Stir in cilantro and sesame oil just before serving.

Per serving (1½ cups): 224 Cal, 8 g Total Fat, 1 g Sat Fat, 0 g Trans Fat, 0 mg Chol, 458 mg Sod, 33 Carb, 6 g Sugar, 5 g Fib, 10 g Prot, 194 mg Calc.

FYI To prepare kale, remove the tough ribs running up the middle of each leaf with a sharp knife. Then roll the leaves like cigars and cut into thin slices.

black bean chili with peppers and anise

serves 6

1 tablespoon olive oil

▲ **2 onions, finely chopped**

4 garlic cloves, minced

½ teaspoon anise seeds, crushed

¼ teaspoon cayenne

▲ **3 (15-ounce) cans black beans, rinsed and drained**

▲ **2 cups reduced-sodium vegetable broth**

▲ **1 (14½-ounce) can diced tomatoes**

▲ **1 red bell pepper, diced**

▲ **2 tablespoons cornmeal**

¼ teaspoon salt

¾ cup fresh cilantro leaves

▲ **2 scallions, thinly sliced**

1 Heat oil in large nonstick skillet over medium heat. Add onions and cook, stirring frequently, until softened, 5 minutes. Stir in garlic, anise seeds, and cayenne; cook, stirring constantly, until fragrant, about 30 seconds. Transfer to 5- or 6-quart slow cooker.

2 Stir in beans, broth, tomatoes, bell pepper, cornmeal, and salt. Cover and cook 4–6 hours on high or 8–10 hours on low. Stir in cilantro and scallions just before serving.

Per serving (1⅓ cups): 284 Cal, 3 g Total Fat, 1 g Sat Fat, 0 g Trans Fat, 0 mg Chol, 839 mg Sod, 51 g Carb, 6 g Sugar, 18 g Fib, 14 g Prot, 146 mg Calc.

CAN'T COMMIT? For a delicious addition to this chili, stir in ¾ pound of ground skinless turkey breast along with the onions in step 1. Cook, stirring to break up the turkey, until browned. Proceed with the recipe. The per-serving *PointsPlus* value will increase by *2*.

curried parsnip soup

serves 6

1 tablespoon canola oil

▲ 1 onion, thinly sliced

2 garlic cloves, thinly sliced

1 teaspoon curry powder

⅛ teaspoon cayenne

▲ 6 cups reduced-sodium vegetable broth

▲ 6 small parsnips (1¼ pounds), peeled and diced

▲ 2 celery stalks, diced

¾ teaspoon salt

1 cup fresh cilantro leaves

▲ ¼ cup fat-free sour cream

1 Heat oil in medium nonstick skillet over medium heat. Add onion and cook, stirring frequently, until softened, about 5 minutes. Add garlic, curry, and cayenne; cook, stirring constantly, until fragrant, about 30 seconds.

2 Transfer mixture to 3- or 4-quart slow cooker. Stir in broth, parsnips, celery, and salt. Cover and cook 4–6 hours on high or 8–10 hours on low. Stir in cilantro just before serving. Ladle into 6 bowls; top evenly with sour cream.

Per serving (1⅓ cups soup and 2 teaspoons sour cream): 110 Cal, 3 g Total Fat, 0 g Sat Fat, 0 g Trans Fat, 1 mg Chol, 761 mg Sod, 21 g Carb, 9 g Sugar, 4 g Fib, 2 g Prot, 63 mg Calc.

STAY ON TRACK Serve this soup with a spinach and mushroom salad to make it a filling meal. Toss together 2 cups baby spinach, 4 thinly sliced white mushrooms, a drizzle of red wine vinegar, and salt and pepper to taste.

asian-style mushroom and greens soup

serves 4

▲ **6 cups reduced-sodium vegetable broth**

▲ **4 cups thinly sliced Napa cabbage**

▲ **6 scallions, thinly sliced**

▲ **12 fresh shiitake mushrooms, stems discarded and caps thinly sliced**

1 tablespoon chopped peeled fresh ginger

2 garlic cloves, halved

¼ teaspoon salt

½ teaspoon whole black peppercorns

▲ **1 cup baby spinach**

½ teaspoon Asian (dark) sesame oil

1 Combine broth, cabbage, scallions, 8 mushrooms, ginger, garlic, salt, and peppercorns in 5- or 6-quart slow cooker. Cover and cook 4–6 hours on high or 8–10 hours on low.

2 Pour through coarse strainer set over large saucepan; press on solids to extract as much liquid as possible. Discard solids. Return soup to slow cooker. Add remaining 4 mushrooms. Cover and cook on high until mushrooms are tender, 10 minutes. Stir in spinach and oil just before serving.

Per serving (1 cup): 82 Cal, 1 g Total Fat, 0 g Sat Fat, 0 g Trans Fat, 0 mg Chol, 811 mg Sod, 19 g Carb, 7 g Sugar, 3 g Fib, 3 g Prot, 98 mg Calc.

CAN'T COMMIT? Add 8 ounces medium peeled and deveined shrimp when you add the remaining mushrooms in step 2. The per-serving **PointsPlus** value will increase by **1**.

sweet potato, green olive, and lemon tagine

serves 4

- ¾ cup reduced-sodium vegetable broth
- Pinch saffron threads, crumbled
- 1 tablespoon olive oil
- 1 red onion, thinly sliced
- 3 garlic cloves, minced
- 2 teaspoons ground coriander
- ½ teaspoon ground ginger
- ¼ teaspoon salt
- ⅛ teaspoon cayenne
- 3 small sweet potatoes (1½ pounds), peeled and cut into ½-inch cubes
- 1 large orange bell pepper, cut into ½-inch pieces
- 2 tablespoons chopped preserved lemon peel
- ¼ cup chopped fresh cilantro
- 4 green olives, pitted and chopped

1 Combine broth and saffron in small bowl. Let stand 5 minutes.

2 Meanwhile, heat oil in medium nonstick skillet over medium heat. Add onion and cook, stirring frequently, until softened, 5 minutes. Add garlic, coriander, ginger, salt, and cayenne. Cook, stirring constantly, until fragrant, about 30 seconds. Transfer to 3- or 4-quart slow cooker.

3 Stir in broth mixture, sweet potatoes, bell pepper, and 1 tablespoon lemon peel. Cover and cook 4–6 hours on high or 8–10 hours on low.

4 Stir in remaining 1 tablespoon lemon peel, cilantro, and olives just before serving.

Per serving (about 1 cup): 172 Cal, 4 g Total Fat, 1 g Sat Fat, 0 g Trans Fat, 0 mg Chol, 413 mg Sod, 32 g Carb, 12 g Sugar, 5 g Fib, 3 g Prot, 67 mg Calc.

FYI If preserved lemon peel is unavailable, you can omit it and stir in 2 teaspoons grated lemon zest just before serving.

SWEET POTATO, GREEN OLIVE, AND LEMON TAGINE

chickpea, squash, and apricot tagine

serves 4

1 tablespoon canola oil
▲ 1 large onion, finely chopped
1 (3-inch) cinnamon stick
2 garlic cloves, minced
½ teaspoon salt
⅛ teaspoon cayenne
▲ 6 cups ½-inch cubes butternut squash
▲ 1 (15-ounce) can chickpeas, rinsed and drained
2 (3-inch) strips orange zest, removed with vegetable peeler
1 cup fresh orange juice
1 cup fresh cilantro leaves
½ cup dried apricot halves, thinly sliced
▲ 2 cups cooked whole wheat couscous
2 tablespoons sliced almonds

1 Heat oil in large nonstick skillet over medium heat. Add onion and cook, stirring frequently, until softened, 5 minutes. Stir in cinnamon stick, garlic, salt, and cayenne. Cook, stirring constantly, until fragrant, about 30 seconds. Transfer to 3- or 4-quart slow cooker.

2 Stir in squash, chickpeas, and orange zest and juice. Cover and cook 4–6 hours on high or 8–10 hours on low. Remove and discard cinnamon stick and orange zest. Stir in cilantro and apricots just before serving. Ladle tagine into 4 bowls. Top each serving with ½ cup couscous and sprinkle evenly with almonds.

Per serving (1½ cups tagine, ½ cup couscous, and ½ tablespoon almonds): 462 Cal, 8 g Total Fat, 1 g Sat Fat, 0 g Trans Fat, 0 mg Chol, 411 mg Sod, 88 g Carb, 25 g Sugar, 17 g Fib, 15 g Prot, 166 mg Calc.

STAY ON TRACK Complete this meal with a simple healthy dessert of sliced fresh strawberries.

lentil and delicata squash tagine

serves 6

1 tablespoon canola oil

▲ 1 large onion, finely chopped

2 tablespoons minced peeled fresh ginger

4 cloves garlic, minced

½ teaspoon salt

⅛ teaspoon cayenne

▲ 1½ cups dried brown lentils, picked over and rinsed

▲ 1 (15-ounce) can black beans, rinsed and drained

▲ 1¾ pounds delicata squash, peeled, seeded, and cut into 1-inch chunks

▲ 2½ cups reduced-sodium vegetable broth

▲ 1 (14½-ounce) can diced tomatoes

▲ 2 (10-ounce) bags frozen broccoli, cauliflower, and carrot blend, thawed

▲ 1 (6-ounce) bag baby spinach

▲ 3 cups cooked whole wheat couscous

1 Heat oil in large nonstick skillet over medium heat. Add onion and cook, stirring frequently, until softened, 5 minutes. Stir in ginger, garlic, salt, and cayenne. Cook, stirring constantly, until fragrant, about 30 seconds. Transfer to 5- or 6-quart slow cooker.

2 Stir in lentils, black beans, squash, broth, and tomatoes. Cover and cook 4–6 hours on high or 8–10 hours on low. Stir in vegetable blend. Cover and cook on high until vegetables are crisp-tender, about 20 minutes. Stir in spinach just before serving. Ladle tagine into 4 bowls. Top each serving with ½ cup couscous.

Per serving (1½ cups tagine and ½ cup couscous): 443 Cal, 4 g Total Fat, 0 g Sat Fat, 0 g Trans Fat, 0 mg Chol, 666 mg Sod, 83 g Carb, 8 g Sugar, 23 g Fib, 23 g Prot, 155 mg Calc.

FYI Delicata is an oval-shaped pale yellow squash with thin green stripes. It is an heirloom variety that fell out of favor because its delicate skin made it difficult to ship. If you can't find it, you can use butternut squash in this recipe.

recipes by *PointsPlus* value

recipes that work with the simply filling technique

index

V

Dry and Liquid Measurement Equivalents

If you are converting the recipes in this book to metric measurements, use the following chart as a guide.

TEASPOONS	TABLESPOONS	CUPS		FLUID OUNCES
3 teaspoons	1 tablespoon			½ fluid ounce
6 teaspoons	2 tablespoons	⅛	cup	1 fluid ounce
8 teaspoons	2 tablespoons plus 2 teaspoons	⅙	cup	
12 teaspoons	4 tablespoons	¼	cup	2 fluid ounces
15 teaspoons	5 tablespoons	⅓	cup minus 1 teaspoon	
16 teaspoons	5 tablespoons plus 1 teaspoon	⅓	cup	
18 teaspoons	6 tablespoons	¼	cup plus 2 tablespoons	3 fluid ounces
24 teaspoons	8 tablespoons	½	cup	4 fluid ounces
30 teaspoons	10 tablespoons	½	cup plus 2 tablespoons	5 fluid ounces
32 teaspoons	10 tablespoons plus 2 teaspoons	⅔	cup	
36 teaspoons	12 tablespoons	¾	cup	6 fluid ounces
42 teaspoons	14 tablespoons	1	cup minus 2 tablespoons	7 fluid ounces
45 teaspoons	15 tablespoons	1	cup minus 1 tablespoon	
48 teaspoons	16 tablespoons	1	cup	8 fluid ounces

VOLUME		
¼ teaspoon	1	milliliter
½ teaspoon	2	milliliters
1 teaspoon	5	milliliters
1 tablespoon	15	milliliters
2 tablespoons	30	milliliters
3 tablespoons	45	milliliters
¼ cup	60	milliliters
⅓ cup	80	milliliters
½ cup	120	milliliters
⅔ cup	160	milliliters
¾ cup	175	milliliters
1 cup	240	milliliters
1 quart	950	milliliters

LENGTH		
1 inch	25	millimeters
1 inch	2.5	centimeters

OVEN TEMPERATURE			
250°F	120°C	400°F	200°C
275°F	140°C	425°F	220°C
300°F	150°C	450°F	230°C
325°F	160°C	475°F	250°C
350°F	180°C	500°F	260°C
375°F	190°C	525°F	270°C

WEIGHT		
1 ounce	30	grams
¼ pound	120	grams
½ pound	240	grams
1 pound	480	grams

Note: Measurement of less than ⅛ teaspoon is considered a dash or a pinch. Metric volume measurements are approximate.